Get Ready!
FOR STANDARDIZED TESTS

MATH, GRADE THREE

Other Books in the *Get Ready!* Series:

Get Ready! for Standardized Tests: Grade 1 by Joseph Harris, Ph.D.

Get Ready! for Standardized Tests: Grade 2 by Joseph Harris, Ph. D.

Get Ready! for Standardized Tests: Grade 3 by Karen Mersky, Ph.D.

Get Ready! for Standardized Tests: Grade 4 by Joseph Harris, Ph.D.

Get Ready! for Standardized Tests: Grade 5 by Leslie E. Talbott, Ph.D.

Get Ready! for Standardized Tests: Grade 6 by Shirley Vickery, Ph.D.

Get Ready! for Standardized Tests: Math, Grade 1 by Sandy McConnell

Get Ready! for Standardized Tests: Math, Grade 2 by Kristin Swanson

Get Ready! for Standardized Tests: Math, Grade 4 by June Heller

Get Ready! for Standardized Tests: Reading, Grade 1 by Molly Maack

Get Ready! for Standardized Tests: Reading, Grade 2 by Louise Ulrich

Get Ready! for Standardized Tests: Reading, Grade 3 by Joanne Baker

Get Ready! for Standardized Tests: Reading, Grade 4 by Kris Callahan

TEST PREPARATION SERIES

Get Ready!
FOR STANDARDIZED TESTS

MATH, GRADE THREE

Susan Osborne

Carol Turkington
Series Editor

McGraw-Hill

New York   Chicago   San Francisco
Lisbon   London   Madrid   Mexico City
Milan   New Delhi   San Juan   Seoul
Singapore   Sydney   Toronto

Library of Congress Cataloging-in-Publication Data

Get ready! for standardized tests. Math.
    p. cm.—(Test preparation series)
  Includes bibliographical references.
  Contents: [1] Grade 1 / Sandy McConnell—[2] Grade 2 / Kristin Swanson—[3] Grade 3 / Susan Osborne—[4] Grade 4 / June Heller
    ISBN 0-07-137399-3 (pbk. : v. 1)—ISBN 0-07-137400-0 (pbk. : v. 2)—ISBN 0-07-137403-5 (pbk. : v. 3)—ISBN 0-07-137404-3 (pbk. : v. 4)
  1. Mathematics—Study and teaching (Elementary)—United States.
  2. Mathematics—Study and teaching—Parent participation—United States. 3. Achievement tests—United States—Study guides.   I. McConnell, Sandy.   II. Test preparation series (McGraw-Hill Companies)

  QA135.6 .G47   2001
  372.7—dc21   2001030901

McGraw-Hill

A Division of The **McGraw·Hill** Companies

Copyright © 2001 by The McGraw-Hill Companies, Inc. All rights reserved. Printed in the United States of America. Except as permitted under the United States Copyright Act of 1976, no part of this publication may be reproduced or distributed in any form or by any means, or stored in a data base or retrieval system, without the prior written permission of the publisher.

1 2 3 4 5 6 7 8 9 0 COU/COU 0 9 8 7 6 5 4 3 2 1

ISBN 0-07-137403-5

This book was set in New Century Schoolbook by Inkwell Publishing Services.

Printed and bound by Courier.

McGraw-Hill books are available at special quantity discounts to use as premiums and sales promotions, or for use in corporate training programs. For more information, please write to the Director of Special Sales, McGraw-Hill, Professional Publishing, Two Penn Plaza, New York, NY 10121-2298. Or contact your local bookstore.

To my daughter Charlotte and my aunt Patricia Bigg for encouraging me to undertake this project; my husband John for his unfailing support throughout; and all the third graders I have had the pleasure to teach over the past thirty years and from whom I have learned so much.

Susan Osborne

MATH, GRADE THREE

Contents

Skills Checklist ix

Introduction 1
Types of Standardized Tests 1
The Major Standardized Tests 2
How States Use Standardized Tests 2
Valid Uses of Standardized
 Test Scores 3
Inappropriate Use of Standardized
 Test Scores 3
Two Basic Assumptions 4
A Word about Coaching 4
How to Raise Test Scores 4
Test Questions 5

Chapter 1. Test-Taking Basics 7
What This Book Can Do 7
How to Use This Book 7
Basic Test-Taking Strategies 8
On to the Second Chapter 8

Chapter 2. Basic Number Facts 11
What Third Graders Should Know 11
What You and Your Child Can Do 12
What Tests May Ask 13
Practice Skill: Basic Facts 13

Chapter 3. Addition 15
What Third Graders Should Know 15
What You and Your Child Can Do 16
What Tests May Ask 17
Practice Skill: Addition 17

Chapter 4. Subtraction 19
What Third Graders Should Know 19
What You and Your Child Can Do 19
What Tests May Ask 20
Practice Skill: Subtraction 21

Chapter 5. Multiplication 23
What Third Graders Should Know 23
What You and Your Child Can Do 24
What Tests May Ask 25
Practice Skill: Multiplication 25

Chapter 6. Division 27
What Third Graders Should Know 27
What You and Your Child Can Do 28
What Tests May Ask 29
Practice Skill: Division 29
Practice Skill: Division with Remainders 30

Chapter 7. Fractions and Decimals 31
Fractions 31
 What Third Graders Should Know 31
 What You and Your Child Can Do 32
 What Tests May Ask 32
 Practice Skill: Fractions 33

Decimals 33
  What Third Graders Should Know 34
  What You and Your Child Can Do 34
  What Tests May Ask 34
  Practice Skill: Decimals 34

Chapter 8. Place Value, Number Sense, and Money   37

What Third Graders Should Know 37
  Missing Numbers 37
  Ordinal Numbers 38
  Rounding 38
What You and Your Child Can Do 39
What Tests May Ask 40
Practice Skill: Place Value, Number Sense, and Money 40

Chapter 9. Geometry   43

What Third Graders Should Know 44
What You and Your Child Can Do 44
What Tests May Ask 45
Practice Skill: Geometry 46
Perimeter, Area, and Volume 47
  What You and Your Child Can Do 48
  What Tests May Ask 49
  Practice Skill: Perimeter, Area, and Volume 49

Chapter 10. Measurements   51

What Third Graders Should Know 51
What You and Your Child Can Do 52
What Tests May Ask 54
Practice Skill: Measurement 54

Chapter 11. Problem Solving   57

What Third Graders Should Know 57
What You and Your Child Can Do 59

What Tests May Ask 60
Practice Skill: Problem Solving 60

Appendix A: Web Sites and Resources for More Information   63

Appendix B: Read More about It   67

Appendix C: What Your Child's Test Scores Mean   69

Appendix D: Which States Require Which Tests   77

Appendix E: Testing Accommodations   87

Glossary   89

Answer Keys for Practice Skills   91

Sample Practice Test   93

Answer Key for Sample Practice Test   122

MATH, GRADE THREE
SKILLS CHECKLIST

MY CHILD ...	HAS LEARNED	IS WORKING ON
BASIC NUMBER FACTS		
ADDITION WITHOUT REGROUPING		
ADDITION WITH REGROUPING		
ESTIMATION		
SUBTRACTION—TWO-DIGIT NUMBERS		
SUBTRACTION—THREE-DIGIT NUMBERS		
SUBTRACTION WITH REGROUPING		
MULTIPLICATION FACTS		
MULTIPLYING ONE-DIGIT NUMBERS		
MULTIPLYING TWO-DIGIT NUMBERS		
SIMPLE DIVISION WITHOUT REMAINDERS		
SIMPLE DIVISION WITH REMAINDERS		
FRACTIONS: ADDING		
FRACTIONS: SUBTRACTING		
DECIMALS		
PLACE VALUE		
MISSING NUMBERS		
ORDINAL NUMBERS		
ROUNDING		
MONEY		
TWO-DIMENSIONAL FIGURES		
THREE-DIMENSIONAL FIGURES		
LINES AND ANGLES		
PATTERNS		
PERIMETER		
AREA		
VOLUME		
STANDARD MEASUREMENTS		
METRIC MEASUREMENTS		
WORD PROBLEMS		

Introduction

Almost all of us have taken standardized tests in school. We spent several days bubbling-in answers, shifting in our seats. No one ever told us why we took the tests or what they would do with the results. We just took them and never heard about them again.

Today many parents aren't aware they are entitled to see their children's permanent records and, at a reasonable cost, to obtain copies of any information not protected by copyright, including testing scores. Late in the school year, most parents receive standardized test results with confusing bar charts and detailed explanations of scores that few people seem to understand.

In response to a series of negative reports on the state of education in this country, Americans have begun to demand that something be done to improve our schools. We have come to expect higher levels of accountability as schools face the competing pressures of rising educational expectations and declining school budgets. High-stakes standardized tests are rapidly becoming the main tool of accountability for students, teachers, and school administrators. If students' test scores don't continually rise, teachers and principals face the potential loss of school funding and, ultimately, their jobs. Summer school and private after-school tutorial program enrollments are swelling with students who have not met score standards or who, everyone agrees, could score higher.

While there is a great deal of controversy about whether it is appropriate for schools to use standardized tests to make major decisions about individual students, it appears likely that standardized tests are here to stay. They will be used to evaluate students, teachers, and the schools; schools are sure to continue to use students' test scores to demonstrate their accountability to the community.

The purposes of this guide are to acquaint you with the types of standardized tests your children may take; to help you understand the test results; and to help you work with your children in skill areas that are measured by standardized tests so they can perform as well as possible.

Types of Standardized Tests

The two major types of group standardized tests are *criterion-referenced tests* and *norm-referenced tests*. Think back to when you learned to tie your shoes. First Mom or Dad showed you how to loosen the laces on your shoe so that you could insert your foot; then they showed you how to tighten the laces—but not too tight. They showed you how to make bows and how to tie a knot. All the steps we just described constitute what is called a *skills hierarchy:* a list of skills from easiest to most difficult that are related to some goal, such as tying a shoelace.

Criterion-referenced tests are designed to determine at what level students are performing on various skills hierarchies. These tests assume that development of skills follows a sequence of steps. For example, if you were teaching shoelace tying, the skills hierarchy might appear this way:

1. Loosen laces.
2. Insert foot.
3. Tighten laces.
4. Make loops with both lace ends.
5. Tie a square knot.

Criterion-referenced tests try to identify how far along the skills hierarchy the student has progressed. There is no comparison against anyone else's score, only against an expected skill level. The main question criterion-referenced tests ask is: "Where is this child in the development of this group of skills?"

Norm-referenced tests, in contrast, are typically constructed to compare children in their abilities as to different skills areas. Although the experts who design test items may be aware of skills hierarchies, they are more concerned with how much of some skill the child has mastered, rather than at what level on the skills hierarchy the child is.

Ideally, the questions on these tests range from very easy items to those that are impossibly difficult. The essential feature of norm-referenced tests is that scores on these measures can be compared to scores of children in similar groups. They answer this question: "How does the child compare with other children of the same age or grade placement in the development of this skill?"

This book provides strategies for increasing your child's scores on both standardized norm-referenced and criterion-referenced tests.

The Major Standardized Tests

Many criterion-referenced tests currently in use are created locally or (at best) on a state level, and there are far too many of them to go into detail here about specific tests. However, children prepare for them in basically the same way they do for norm-referenced tests.

A very small pool of norm-referenced tests is used throughout the country, consisting primarily of the Big Five:

- California Achievement Tests (CTB/McGraw-Hill)
- Iowa Tests of Basic Skills (Riverside)
- Metropolitan Achievement Test (Harcourt-Brace & Company)
- Stanford Achievement Test (Psychological Corporation)
- TerraNova [formerly Comprehensive Test of Basic Skills] (McGraw-Hill)

These tests use various terms for the academic skills areas they assess, but they generally test several types of reading, language, and mathematics skills, along with social studies and science. They may include additional assessments, such as of study and reference skills.

How States Use Standardized Tests

Despite widespread belief and practice to the contrary, group standardized tests are designed to assess and compare the achievement of groups. They are *not* designed to provide detailed diagnostic assessments of individual students. (For detailed individual assessments, children should be given individual diagnostic tests by properly qualified professionals, including trained guidance counselors, speech and language therapists, and school psychologists.) Here are examples of the types of questions group standardized tests are designed to answer:

- How did the reading achievement of students at Valley Elementary School this year compare with their reading achievement last year?

INTRODUCTION

- How did math scores at Wonderland Middle School compare with those of students at Parkside Middle School this year?
- As a group, how did Hilltop High School students compare with the national averages in the achievement areas tested?
- How did the district's first graders' math scores compare with the district's fifth graders' math scores?

The fact that these tests are designed primarily to test and compare groups doesn't mean that test data on individual students isn't useful. It does mean that when we use these tests to diagnose individual students, we are using them for a purpose for which they were not designed.

Think of group standardized tests as being similar to health fairs at the local mall. Rather than check into your local hospital and spend thousands of dollars on full, individual tests for a wide range of conditions, you can go from station to station and take part in different health screenings. Of course, one would never diagnose heart disease or cancer on the basis of the screening done at the mall. At most, suspicious results on the screening would suggest that you need to visit a doctor for a more complete examination.

In the same way, group standardized tests provide a way of screening the achievement of many students quickly. Although you shouldn't diagnose learning problems solely based on the results of these tests, the results can tell you that you should think about referring a child for a more definitive, individual assessment.

An individual student's group test data should be considered only a point of information. Teachers and school administrators may use standardized test results to support or question hypotheses they have made about students; but these scores must be used alongside other information, such as teacher comments, daily work, homework, class test grades, parent observations, medical needs, and social history.

Valid Uses of Standardized Test Scores

Here are examples of appropriate uses of test scores for individual students:

- Mr. Cone thinks that Samantha, a third grader, is struggling in math. He reviews her file and finds that her first- and second-grade standardized test math scores were very low. Her first- and second-grade teachers recall episodes in which Samantha cried because she couldn't understand certain math concepts, and mention that she was teased by other children, who called her "Dummy." Mr. Cone decides to refer Samantha to the school assistance team to determine whether she should be referred for individual testing for a learning disability related to math.

- The local college wants to set up a tutoring program for elementary school children who are struggling academically. In deciding which youngsters to nominate for the program, the teachers consider the students' averages in different subjects, the degree to which students seem to be struggling, parents' reports, and standardized test scores.

- For the second year in a row, Gene has performed poorly on the latest round of standardized tests. His teachers all agree that Gene seems to have some serious learning problems. They had hoped that Gene was immature for his class and that he would do better this year; but his dismal grades continue. Gene is referred to the school assistance team to determine whether he should be sent to the school psychologist for assessment of a possible learning handicap.

Inappropriate Use of Standardized Test Scores

Here are examples of how schools have sometimes used standardized test results inappropriately:

- Mr. Johnson groups his students into reading groups solely on the basis of their standardized test scores.
- Ms. Henry recommends that Susie be held back a year because she performed poorly on the standardized tests, despite strong grades on daily assignments, homework, and class tests.
- Gerald's teacher refers him for consideration in the district's gifted program, which accepts students using a combination of intelligence test scores, achievement test scores, and teacher recommendations. Gerald's intelligence test scores were very high. Unfortunately, he had a bad cold during the week of the standardized group achievement tests and was taking powerful antihistamines, which made him feel sleepy. As a result, he scored too low on the achievement tests to qualify.

The public has come to demand increasingly high levels of accountability for public schools. We demand that schools test so that we have hard data with which to hold the schools accountable. But too often, politicians and the public place more faith in the test results than is justified. Regardless of whether it's appropriate to do so and regardless of the reasons schools use standardized test results as they do, many schools base crucial programming and eligibility decisions on scores from group standardized tests. It's to your child's advantage, then, to perform as well as possible on these tests.

Two Basic Assumptions

The strategies we present in this book come from two basic assumptions:

1. Most students can raise their standardized test scores.
2. Parents can help their children become stronger in the skills the tests assess.

This book provides the information you need to learn what skill areas the tests measure, what general skills your child is being taught in a particular grade, how to prepare your child to take the tests, and what to do with the results. In the appendices you will find information to help you decipher test interpretations; a listing of which states currently require what tests; and additional resources to help you help your child to do better in school and to prepare for the tests.

A Word about Coaching

This guide is *not* about coaching your child. When we use the term *coaching* in referring to standardized testing, we mean trying to give someone an unfair advantage, either by revealing beforehand what exact items will be on the test or by teaching "tricks" that will supposedly allow a student to take advantage of some detail in how the tests are constructed.

Some people try to coach students in shrewd test-taking strategies that take advantage of how the tests are supposedly constructed rather than strengthening the students' skills in the areas tested. Over the years, for example, many rumors have been floated about "secret formulas" that test companies use.

This type of coaching emphasizes ways to help students obtain scores they didn't earn—to get something for nothing. Stories have appeared in the press about teachers who have coached their students on specific questions, parents who have tried to obtain advance copies of tests, and students who have written down test questions after taking standardized tests and sold them to others. Because of the importance of test security, test companies and states aggressively prosecute those who attempt to violate test security—and they should do so.

How to Raise Test Scores

Factors that are unrelated to how strong students are but that might artificially lower test scores include anything that prevents students from making scores that accurately describe their actual abilities. Some of those factors are:

- giving the tests in uncomfortably cold or hot rooms;
- allowing outside noises to interfere with test taking; and
- reproducing test booklets in such small print or with such faint ink that students can't read the questions.

Such problems require administrative attention from both the test publishers, who must make sure that they obtain their norms for the tests under the same conditions students face when they take the tests; and school administrators, who must ensure that conditions under which their students take the tests are as close as possible to those specified by the test publishers.

Individual students also face problems that can artificially lower their test scores, and parents can do something about many of these problems. Stomach aches, headaches, sleep deprivation, colds and flu, and emotional upsets due to a recent tragedy are problems that might call for the student to take the tests during make-up sessions. Some students have physical conditions such as muscle-control problems, palsies, or difficulty paying attention that require work over many months or even years before students can obtain accurate test scores on standardized tests. And, of course, some students just don't take the testing seriously or may even intentionally perform poorly. Parents can help their children overcome many of these obstacles to obtaining accurate scores.

Finally, with this book parents are able to help their children raise their scores by:

- increasing their familiarity (and their comfort level) with the types of questions on standardized tests;
- drills and practice exercises to increase their skill in handling the kinds of questions they will meet; and
- providing lots of fun ways for parents to help their children work on the skill areas that will be tested.

Test Questions

The favorite type of question for standardized tests is the multiple-choice question. For example:

1. The first President of the United States was:

   A Abraham Lincoln

   B Martin Luther King, Jr.

   C George Washington

   D Thomas Jefferson

The main advantage of multiple-choice questions is that it is easy to score them quickly and accurately. They lend themselves to optical scanning test forms, on which students fill in bubbles or squares and the forms are scored by machine. Increasingly, companies are moving from paper-based testing to computer-based testing, using multiple-choice questions.

The main disadvantage of multiple-choice questions is that they restrict test items to those that can be put in that form. Many educators and civil rights advocates have noted that the multiple-choice format only reveals a superficial understanding of the subject. It's not possible with multiple-choice questions to test a student's ability to construct a detailed, logical argument on some issue or to explain a detailed process. Although some of the major tests are beginning to incorporate more subjectively scored items, such as short answer or essay questions, the vast majority of test items continue to be in multiple-choice format.

In the past, some people believed there were special formulas or tricks to help test-takers determine which multiple-choice answer was the correct one. There may have been some truth to *some* claims for past tests. Computer analyses of some past tests revealed certain biases in how tests were constructed. For example, the old advice to pick *D* when in doubt appears to have been valid for some past tests. However, test publishers have become so sophisticated in their ability to detect patterns of bias in the formulation of test questions and answers that they now guard against it aggressively.

In Chapter 1, we provide information about general test-taking considerations, with advice on how parents can help students overcome testing obstacles. The rest of the book provides information to help parents help their children strengthen skills in the tested areas.

Joseph Harris, Ph.D.

CHAPTER 1

Test-Taking Basics

At some point during the 12 years that your children spend in school, they'll face a standardized testing situation. Some schools test every year, and some test every other year—but at some point your child will be assessed. How well your child does on such a test can be related to many things—did he get plenty of rest the night before? Is he anxious in testing situations? Did he get confused when filling in the answer sheets and make a mechanical mistake?

That's why educators emphasize that a child's score on a standardized test shouldn't be used as the sole judge of how that child is learning and developing. Instead, the scores should be evaluated as only one part of the educational picture, together with the child's classroom performance and overall areas of strength and weakness. Your child won't pass or fail a standardized test, but you can often see a general pattern of strengths and weaknesses.

What This Book Can Do

This book is not designed to help your child artificially inflate scores on a standardized test. Instead, it's to help you understand the typical kinds of skills taught in a third-grade class and what a typical third grader can be expected to know by the end of the year. It also presents lots of fun activities that you can use at home to work with your child in particular skill areas that may be a bit weak.

Of course, this book should not be used to replace your child's teacher but as a guide to help you work together with the school as a team to help your child succeed. Keep in mind, however, that endless drilling is not the best way to help your child improve. While most children want to do well and please their teachers and parents, they already spend about 7 hours a day in school. Extracurricular activities, homework, music, and play take up more time. Try to use the activities in this book to stimulate and support your children's work at school, not to overwhelm them.

Most children in third grade are eager to learn. There's certainly nothing wrong with working with your child, but if you're trying to teach the same skill over and over and your child just isn't "getting it," you may be trying to teach something that your child just isn't ready for. Remember that not all children learn things at the same rate. What may be typical for one third grader is certainly not typical for another. You should use the information presented in this book in conjunction with school work to help develop your child's essential skills in mathematics and numbers.

How to Use This Book

There are many different ways to use this book. Some children are quite strong in certain math areas but need a bit of help in other areas. Perhaps your child is a whiz at adding but has more trouble with telling time. Focus your attention on those skills which need some work, and spend more time on those areas.

You'll see in each chapter an introductory explanation of the material in the chapter, followed by a summary of what a typical child in third grade should be expected to know about that skill by the end of the year. This is followed in each chapter by an extensive section featuring interesting, fun, or unusual activities you can do with your child to reinforce the skills presented in the chapter. Most use only inexpensive items found around the home, and many are suitable for car trips, waiting rooms, and restaurants. Next, you'll find an explanation of how typical standardized tests may assess the skill in question and what your child might expect to see on a typical test.

We've included sample questions at the end of each section that are designed to help familiarize your child with the types of questions found on a typical standardized test. These questions do *not* measure your child's proficiency in any given content area—but if you notice that your child is having trouble with a particular question, you can use that information to figure out what skills you need to focus on.

Basic Test-Taking Strategies

Sometimes children score lower on standardized tests because they approach testing in an inefficient way. There are things you can do before the test—and that your child can do during the test—to make sure he does as well as he can.

There are a few things you might want to remember about standardized tests. One is that they can only ask a limited number of questions dealing with each skill before they run out of paper. On most tests, the total math component is made up of about 60 items and takes about 90 minutes. In some cases, your child may encounter only one exercise evaluating a particular skill. An important practice area that is often overlooked is the *listening* element of the tests. Most of the math questions are done as a group and are read to the students by the proctor of the test, who is almost always the classroom teacher.

You can practice this by reading the directions to each question to your third grader. Sometimes the instructions are so brief and to the point that they are almost too simple. In some cases, teachers are not permitted to reword or explain, they may only read what is written in the test manual. Read the directions as they have been given on the practice pages, and then have your child explain to you what they mean. Then you'll both be clear about what the tests actually require.

Before the Test
Perhaps the most effective thing you can do to prepare your child for standardized tests is to be patient. Remember that no matter how much pressure you put on your children, they won't learn certain skills until they are physically, mentally, and emotionally ready to do so. You've got to walk a delicate line between challenging and pressuring your children. If you see that your child isn't making progress or is getting frustrated, it may be time to lighten up.

Don't Change the Routine. Many experts offer mistaken advice about how to prepare children for a test, such as recommending that children go to bed early the night before or eat a high-protein breakfast on the morning of the test. It's a better idea not to alter your child's routine at all right before the test.

If your child isn't used to going to bed early, then sending him off at 7:30 p.m. the night before a test will only make it harder for him to get to sleep by the normal time. If he is used to eating an orange or a piece of toast for breakfast, forcing him to down a platter of fried eggs and bacon will only make him feel sleepy or uncomfortable.

Neatness. There is an incorrect way to fill in an answer sheet on a standardized test, and if this happens to your child, it can really make a difference on the final results. It pays to give your child some practice filling in answer sheets. Watch how neatly your child can fill in the bubbles, squares, and rectangles on the following page. If he overlaps the lines, makes a lot of

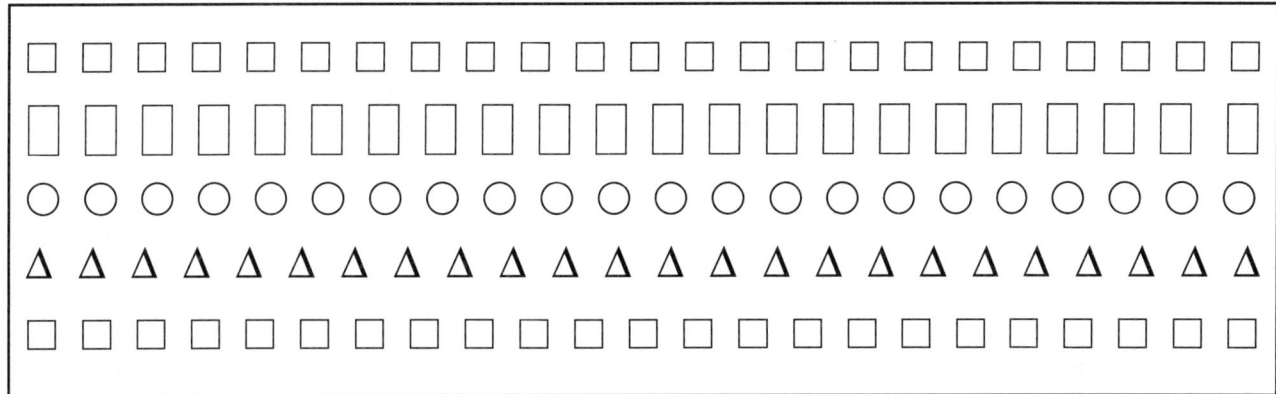

erase marks, or presses the pencil too hard, try having him practice with pages of bubbles. You can easily create sheets of capital O's, squares, and rectangles that your child can practice filling in. If he gets bored doing that, have him color in detailed pictures in coloring books or complete connect-the-dots pages.

During the Test

There are some approaches to standardized testing that have been shown to make some degree of improvement in a score. Discuss the following strategies with your child from time to time.

Bring Extra Pencils. You don't want your child spending valuable testing time jumping up to sharpen a pencil. Send along plenty of extra, well-sharpened pencils, and your child will have more time to work on test questions.

Listen Carefully. You wouldn't believe how many errors children make by not listening to instructions or not paying attention to demonstrations. Some children mark the wrong form, fill in the bubbles incorrectly, or skip to the wrong section. Others simply forget to put their names on the answer sheets. Many make a mark on the answer sheet without realizing whether they are marking the right bubble.

Read the Entire Question First. Some children get so excited about the test that they begin filling in bubbles before they finish reading the entire question. The last few words in a question sometimes give the most important clues to the correct answer.

Read Carefully. In their desire to finish first, many children tend to select the first answer that seems right to them without thoroughly reading all the responses and choosing the very best answer. Make sure your child understands the importance of evaluating all the answers before choosing one.

Skip Difficult Items; Return Later. Many children will sit and worry about a hard question, spending so much time on one problem that they never get to problems that they would be able to answer correctly if they only had left enough time. Explain to your child that he can always come back to a knotty question once he finishes the section.

Use Key Words. Have your child look at the questions and try to figure out the parts that are important and those which aren't.

Eliminate Answer Choices. Just like in the wildly successful TV show *Who Wants to Be a Millionaire,* remind your child that it's a good idea to narrow down his choices among multiple-choice options by eliminating answers he knows can't possibly be true.

On to the Second Chapter

Now that you've learned a bit about the test-taking basics, it's time to turn your attention to the first of the math skills—number basics.

CHAPTER 2

Basic Number Facts

Traditionally, the first weeks of third grade are spent reviewing the basic addition and subtraction facts as well as simple addition and subtraction of two- and three-digit numbers. Many students already will have been exposed to the process of regrouping in addition problems—and perhaps subtraction, too. (*Regrouping* is the modern mathematical term used for what used to be called *carrying* or *borrowing*.)

Students will then move on to more complex problems where regrouping is used more than once in a problem and four- or even five-digit numbers are used. Learning to apply the correct processes to solve word problems is an important part of the curriculum and is an ongoing process.

As the year proceeds, these problems will become increasingly complex and will require students to go through a number of steps to arrive at the answers. In addition to straightforward computation and word problems, your child probably will have "hands-on" activities where she will solve various life-relevant problems, often with a partner or group. The use of calculators is encouraged these days, particularly when students are dealing with very large numbers and complex, multistep problems.

What Third Graders Should Know

Many third graders know their basic addition and subtraction facts up to 20, applying them rapidly and accurately on entering third grade and quickly moving on to more advanced procedures. However, after the long summer vacation, many students become rusty and slow, often pausing before they respond or even counting on their fingers before they come up with the answer. They will need to review and practice to brush up on their skills. Some children will require constant review throughout the year. It is of utmost importance that your child really knows these basic facts in order to move smoothly forward on to more challenging procedures.

As you help your child, you might become a little confused when you're first confronted with modern math terminology. In the basic fact $5 + 7 = 12$, 5 and 7 are the *addends*, and 12 is referred to as the *sum*. The answer 9 in the subtraction fact $17 - 8 = 9$ is referred to as the *difference*.

Addition facts usually are easier for most children to master than subtraction facts. They should be able to understand that the order of the addends in an addition fact does not affect the sum. (For example, $8 + 9 = 17$, and $9 + 8 = 17$.) However, it's essential that your child learn that the order of the numbers is very important in subtraction. For example, it doesn't make sense to write $8 - 17 = 9$, but it does make sense to write $17 - 8 = 9$.

Students need to grasp the concept that addition is the opposite of subtraction. Learning the various fact families is often one way to do this. Usually, a fact family uses three numbers to show two different addition facts and two different subtraction facts.

Example: Numbers: 8, 7, and 15.

8 + 7 = 15   15 − 8 = 7
7 + 8 = 15   15 − 7 = 8

When only two different numbers are involved, as in the case of 6 and 12, obviously there will be only two facts to learn.

Example: 6 + 6 = 12   12 − 6 = 6

Students learn to recognize that an addition fact can help you find the difference between two numbers.

Example: 13 − 5 = ? Think 5 + ? = 13, and of course, the missing addend is 8.

Students also should be comfortable adding more than two numbers at a time. They learn to group addends in different ways to come up with a sum quickly. They are encouraged to look for numbers that add up to 10 or to look for doubles of a number.

Learning how to select and apply correct addition and subtraction facts to solve oral or written word problems helps students think mathematically. This skill will be carried on when they move on to more complicated addition and subtraction word problems.

What You and Your Child Can Do

Over the summer before your child enters third grade, it would be wise to review the basic facts in a nonthreatening situation. If there have been real problems in this area, it is very likely that your child's second-grade teacher already will have informed you. However, most children will benefit from brushing up on their facts. Either giving your child a written inventory or just asking her facts out loud will give you a good measure of what she knows. Often there are just a few facts that cause problems, or you discover that her retrieval is slow and she needs to pick up the pace.

Try practicing in the car or in spare moments during the day while doing routine chores. This can provide an ideal opportunity to review, practice, and pick up on retrieval time! Ideally, your child should get to a point where the response is instantaneous. It's important to make a game out of the process and avoid making it seem like work. It's all too easy to turn a child off completely. Keep the sessions fairly brief but frequent and consistent.

Flash Cards. Some children respond better to visual questions rather than verbal ones. Ideally, they should become proficient at both. You can buy flash cards with the basic addition or subtraction fact on the front and the answer on the back. These days there are even three-corner flash cards and math wheel cards to choose from. You can buy them at any local educational products store that caters to the needs of parents and teachers.

Make Your Own Cards. Why not let your child make her own flash cards? You'll need index cards, and colored markers or pencils. This can be a very worthwhile experience as well as being a fun activity!

Model It. If your child is finding the process laborious, you'll need to slow down the pace. Using beads, buttons, beans, or plastic counters, you can model the fact before your child writes it down. It can be helpful to work through one fact family—First model the addition facts and then make the number cards to go with them. Next, model the subtraction facts with the manipulatives, and finally make the subtraction flash cards. This will help reinforce the facts in a logical manner. These activities and the practice your child will get using the flash cards with you afterwards may be all that your child can cope with in one session. Other children may feel comfortable dealing with more than one fact family.

Domino Add. An easy way to practice basic facts is to use a box of dominoes and add the two

BASIC NUMBER FACTS

sides of a domino. To practice subtraction, let your child come up with her own fact by taking the smaller number away from the larger. You and your child could devise your own game on this theme. Bingo is another game that can be adapted very easily to learning basic facts.

Computer Games. These days, most homes have computers, and children are wonderfully adept at using them. There are various excellent computer software programs such as *Math Blaster* and *JumpStart Third Grade* that should make the process of learning math facts fun.

Music Math. If your child responds to music, look for musical math kits with cassettes or CDs designed to help reinforce addition and subtraction basic facts set to music. These kits are lively, fun, and have a catchy beat.

Twist and Shout. This new type of math toy features addition set to a catchy beat with answers that flash on an LCD screen. This interactive learning tool beats flash cards hands down. By twisting the game cylinder, children can add numbers, see answers, and get a little entertainment at the same time. This portable toy includes three games and two skill level quiz modes—a great idea for long car rides or lazy afternoons.

What Tests May Ask

The skills in this chapter appear on standardized tests both as problems presented in isolation and as word problems. Students will be given problems and then asked to choose the correct answer from a number of possibilities.

Practice Skill: Basic Facts

Directions: Read each of the following problems and select the correct answer.

Example:

$$\begin{array}{r} 2 \\ +3 \\ \hline \end{array}$$

Ⓐ 6
Ⓑ 1
Ⓒ 7
Ⓓ 5

Answer:

Ⓓ 5

1. $$\begin{array}{r} 5 \\ +8 \\ \hline \end{array}$$

    Ⓐ 14
    Ⓑ 15
    ● 13
    Ⓓ 12

2. $$\begin{array}{r} 16 \\ -\ 9 \\ \hline \end{array}$$

    Ⓐ 8
    Ⓑ 9
    ● 7
    Ⓓ 25

3. $$\begin{array}{r} 7 \\ 3 \\ +4 \\ \hline \end{array}$$

    Ⓐ 12
    ● 14
    Ⓒ 11
    Ⓓ 13

4 Choose a family of facts for the group of numbers 6, 9, and 15.

- Ⓐ 6 + 9 = 15
  9 + 6 = 15
  24 − 9 = 15
  21 − 6 = 15

- Ⓑ 9 + 6 = 15
  15 + 9 = 24
  6 + 6 = 12
  9 − 6 = 15

- Ⓒ 6 + 9 = 15
  9 + 6 = 15
  15 − 6 = 9
  15 − 9 = 6

- Ⓓ 15 + 9 = 24
  6 + 15 = 21
  9 − 6 = 3
  15 − 9 = 6

5 Find the missing addend:
14 − ___ = 7.

- Ⓐ 5
- Ⓑ 7
- Ⓒ 6
- Ⓓ 14

6 A gray squirrel dug a hole under an oak tree and hid 18 acorns. Later in the day another squirrel came along and dug up 9 of the acorns. He then gobbled them up. How many acorns were left?

- Ⓐ 14
- Ⓑ 16
- Ⓒ 15
- Ⓓ 9

(See page 91 for answer key.)

CHAPTER 3

Addition

By the time your child enters third grade, he will have been spending quite a bit of time on adding, with an emphasis on adding accurately. This year, your child's teachers will begin to expand coverage to include adding with multi-digit numbers with regrouping.

What Third Graders Should Know

Once third graders are secure in their basic facts up to 20 and have a good grasp of the place value of tens of thousands, thousands, hundreds, tens, and ones, they will begin to add two- and three-digit numbers without regrouping. They will quickly move on to a review of regrouping once in a problem. They already will have had practice with this process in second grade.

In many schools, students use place-value charts depicting columns for thousands, hundreds, tens, and ones as well as base 10 blocks to model addition with regrouping.

When you regroup, the ones in the problem indicated below add up to 13, 1 ten and 3 ones. The 1 ten is regrouped to the top of the tens column and added in with the rest of the tens. There is no more regrouping in the problem.

tens	ones
1	
5	4
+3	9
9	3

In the problem below, there are regroupings twice, in both the ones and the tens.

hundreds	tens	ones
1	1	
3	9	6
+2	5	7
6	5	3

The ones add up to 13 ones: 1 ten and 3 ones. The 1 ten is regrouped to the tens column and added onto the 9 and 5 tens, making 15 tens: 1 hundred and 5 tens. The 1 hundred is regrouped to the top of the hundreds column and added to the hundreds. As you can see, the 1 ten and the 1 hundred are indicated at the top of the tens and the hundreds columns by the child so that he doesn't forget to add them on. It's most important that he remember to do this from the very beginning.

There are times when your child may be adding four- and five-digit numbers together, and he will have to regroup three or four times. Students need to know that this will happen when places have a sum of more than 9, as illustrated below.

thousands	hundreds	tens	ones
1	1	1	
7,	6	8	5
+ 9,	6	9	8
17,	3	8	3

Your child also will be expected to add as many as four large numbers together accurately, often with regrouping.

```
   322
   409
   786
+  250
 1,767
```

In recent years, students have been taught to estimate so that they can quickly find answers where an exact answer isn't needed. Words such as *about, approximately,* and *close to* indicate that estimation is used. Estimating is also a useful tool for the student to use to find approximately what the final accurate sum should be. Each number is rounded to the nearest hundred or ten, according to its size, and then added together. Students should become proficient at estimating in their heads.

In third grade, your child will learn that we add amounts of money in the same way that we add other numbers. However, they need to line up the decimal points and remember to put the dollar sign and decimal point in the sum. Frequently, students will have hands-on experiences handling play money or even real money in the classroom situation.

What You and Your Child Can Do

Math in Action! You probably can help your child best by relating addition to his daily life in a casual way. For instance, your child could take along a calculator to the supermarket and keep adding the items up as you drop them in the cart. See if his total is the same as yours at checkout.

Money Talks. Let your child handle real money and become comfortable adding up coins and notes. See that he records amounts correctly with a dollar sign and decimal point. While traveling, it can be fun to add up the mileage as you travel from place to place. Often children can be fascinated by numbers, particularly big ones. You also often can find numbers in newspapers that can be used creatively to construct interesting addition problems.

Master the Facts. Common errors in more challenging addition problems often are caused by shaky basic facts. If a child is not secure in this area, it makes the whole process a lot more frustrating. Look for errors in calculations made from mistakes in this area. You can then help your child master the addition facts with flash cards or other suggestions offered in Chapter 2.

Grid Paper. If your child has trouble correctly lining up his numbers in columns when he copies down problems, this can easily lead to errors. You'll probably know by now if your child has problems dealing with the layout of written work. Using centimeter grid paper for this age group can be a great help. For some children, labeling the columns *thousands, hundreds, tens,* and *ones* might help, too. Encourage your child to leave free rows of squares above, below, and on either side so that his calculations aren't all squashed together.

Make Your Own Grids. If you can't find grid paper, you can always measure out the squares on plain paper and then copy off a pile. Another easy solution is to turn lined paper 90 degrees so that the lines form columns going down the page. This will help your child align digits correctly.

Focus! If your child is working on a page in a workbook and finds it difficult to focus on particular problems, cut out a box shape from a sheet of construction paper to surround the problem being tackled. This will help your child concentrate on the one particular problem and not be distracted by other problems around it.

Checkmate. In school, students are taught to add both up and down as a double-checking precaution. This should become second nature. For some children, this will be a tedious process—but try to encourage the habit when dealing

ADDITION

with complex problems! Sometimes it's okay to let a child check calculations with a calculator to see if he has made any errors. He can then go back and work through the problem again if he finds a mistake.

> **TIP**
>
> Every child develops at a different rate. For some, it's really hard to concentrate consistently and accurately on complex calculations. They might very readily understand the concept and be quite clever in their mathematical thinking but find rows of problems very laborious. Don't overburden your child, but give him a manageable task where he can have a good chance of being successful.

Base 10 Blocks. If your child doesn't fully comprehend the concepts behind addition, you may need to use manipulatives. Borrow or buy a set of base 10 blocks (or you can improvise and make your own set). They need not be three-dimensional; you could easily cut the shapes out of centimeter grid paper and glue them to index cards, which can be laminated. Using these manipulatives with a place-value chart should be a great help. (It might be wise to ask the classroom teacher the exact procedure he or she uses when employing base 10 blocks in the classroom so that the child is not confused.)

What Tests May Ask

Two- and three-digit addition is a math computation skill and is included in that portion of the test. Your child will be asked simply to solve the problems in a certain amount of time and probably to solve some word problems involving two-digit numbers.

Your child may be expected to add two- and three-digit numbers with and without regrouping and solve word problems using two-digit addition with and without regrouping. Children also may be asked to solve problems on scratch paper and transfer the solution to the test page.

Practice Skill: Addition

Directions: Read the following problems and select the correct answer.

Example: Mentally add 100 + 200.

- Ⓐ 200
- Ⓑ 300
- Ⓒ 400
- Ⓓ 100

Answer:

- Ⓑ 300

---

1 Mentally add 400 + 600.
- Ⓐ 100
- Ⓑ 1,000
- Ⓒ 600
- Ⓓ 4,000

---

2 16
   27
   87
 +34
- Ⓐ 154
- Ⓑ 162
- Ⓒ 144
- Ⓓ 164

---

3 Estimate the sum of 768 + 832.
- Ⓐ 1,400
- Ⓑ 160
- Ⓒ 1,600
- Ⓓ 1,500

4 456
  +985

  Ⓐ 1,441
  Ⓑ 1,431
  Ⓒ 1,341
  Ⓓ 1,440

5 $4.36
  + 8.98

  Ⓐ $13.24
  Ⓑ $12.34
  Ⓒ $13.34
  Ⓓ $12.14

6 3,626
  +7,597

  Ⓐ 10,222
  Ⓑ 11,233
  Ⓒ 11,224
  Ⓓ 11,223

7 Simon had 12 oranges. Suzy had 18 oranges. How many oranges were there all together?

  Ⓐ 12
  Ⓑ 6
  Ⓒ 30
  Ⓓ 20

(See page 91 for answer key.)

CHAPTER 4

Subtraction

Much of the beginning of third grade is spent reviewing and refining skills learned in second grade, including the basic subtraction facts and simple subtraction problems consisting of two- and three-digit numbers. Some students already will have been exposed to the regrouping (borrowing) process in second grade, but they'll need plenty of reinforcement. Others will be introduced to it for the first time.

Students usually find subtraction a lot more challenging to contend with than its opposite process—addition. For some children, regrouping can be the most frustrating thing they've ever encountered. It's important for parents to understand that the best way for children to learn math concepts is with a hands-on approach. Kids need to see things in a concrete way before they can comprehend them in their abstract form. Regrouping is a perfect example of this.

What Third Graders Should Know

Third graders are expected to understand how to subtract up to four-digit numbers with regrouping. They learn that they need to regroup to find the answer when they look in the ones place and the top digit is less than the bottom digit. They understand that they will need to exchange 1 ten in the tens column for 10 ones. By doing this, they increase the ones column by 10 ones and decrease the tens column by 1 ten. This process is shown by crossing out the existing numbers on the top row of the problem and recording the exchange. It's very likely that students will be working with place-value charts and base 10 blocks at the beginning of the year so that they can visualize the process and handle the movement of the cubes.

It will be the same process when students are presented with a problem where they will need to regroup in the ones, tens, hundreds, and thousands columns. They understand that they will need to regroup tens, hundreds, and thousands. When you regroup 1 thousand, it becomes 10 hundreds, the same way 1 hundred becomes 10 tens, and 1 ten becomes 10 ones.

Learning to subtract across zeroes is one of the most challenging mathematical procedures students learn in third grade. Many children take the whole year or even longer to grasp the concept fully.

To check to see if their answers are correct, students are taught to add the difference to the bottom line of the subtraction problem. Students are also taught that subtracting money is exactly the same as subtracting whole numbers, except that the cents and dollars are separated by the decimal point and they need a dollar sign in front of the answer.

Estimating differences is also taught so that the child can quickly calculate a subtraction problem when the exact answer isn't needed. Words such as *about, approximately, almost,* and *close to* are often used when estimating.

What You and Your Child Can Do

Graph It! Being insecure in her basic subtraction facts can hold your child back when she is dealing with the complexities of regrouping procedures in subtraction problems. Check to see that your child knows her facts (check back with Chapter 1 for more information on this). Note whether your child is lining up numbers correctly when she is copying problems. Using centimeter graph paper or lined paper turned around so that the lines make columns running down the page will help keep the digits separate. Remind your child to take the time to check her work by adding in the manner described in the preceding section. You may need to help your child by encouraging her to use base 10 blocks and a place-value chart. Watching your child model the regrouping procedures may enable you to spot problems. (The use of place-value charts and base 10 blocks is discussed at some length in Chapter 2 under "What You and Your Child Can Do.")

Time It. For extra practice, give your child six three-digit numbers and see how many subtraction facts she can create and solve. To make the process more like a game, use an egg timer to see how long it takes. You can make this game as easy or as challenging as you think is appropriate.

Compare. Many children in this age group have only recently begun to comprehend large numbers and often are quite intrigued by them. Reach for an encyclopedia or go to the computer and have some fun comparing the world's longest rivers or highest mountains. Comparing the populations of large cities, states, and countries can capture the imagination of children who have a sophisticated appreciation of numbers. Look up the dates of the presidents and calculate which one lived the longest life and who lived the shortest. Find out how many years have passed between the births of George Washington and the current President. The possibilities are endless. Your child probably has some particular passion. Third-grade boys often are becoming fascinated with sports—have him compare records, scores, and so on. The daily newspapers also can be a wonderful source of numbers to be compared. The world's or the country's various temperatures can be lots of fun to compare. For instance, what is the difference in temperature today between the hottest place on earth and the coldest?

What's Your Order? Grab a few takeout restaurant menus that would appeal to your child. Give her a $10 bill and ask her to choose what she would like to order from the menu. She needs to choose things that will be within her budget and be able to calculate how much change she'll get. If possible, have coins for her to handle. This theme could be adapted to various other possibilities. Going on a trip to the supermarket can provide an opportunity for your child to draw up a budget for purchasing certain items and calculating how much change she should get. In this situation, you may wish to let your child use a calculator. Remind your child that you always start with the first digit of a number when entering it in a calculator. Adapt these ideas to suit your circumstances.

What Tests May Ask

Two-, three-, and four-digit subtraction is included in that portion of the standardized test for third grade. Your child will be asked simply to solve problems in a certain amount of time. Children will be expected to subtract two-, three-, and four-digit numbers with regrouping, solve some money-related subtraction problems, and solve word problems using two-, three-, and four-digit subtraction with and without regrouping. Children also may be asked to solve problems on scratch paper and transfer the solution to the test page.

SUBTRACTION

Practice Skill: Subtraction

Directions: Read the following problems and select the correct answer.

Example:

Subtract mentally: 50 − 12 = ___.

- (A) 28
- (B) 38
- (C) 48
- (D) 62

Answer:

- (B) 38

---

1. Subtract mentally: 48 − 12 = ___.
   - (A) 30
   - (B) 28
   - (C) 38
   - (D) 36

---

2. Estimate the difference:
   724 − 382 = ___.
   - (A) 300
   - (B) 342
   - (C) 400
   - (D) 200

---

3. 94
   −37
   - (A) 53
   - (B) 67
   - (C) 57
   - (D) 47

---

4. 600
   −286
   - (A) 314
   - (B) 300
   - (C) 886
   - (D) 324

---

5. $23.60
   − 9.57
   - (A) $13.07
   - (B) $14.13
   - (C) $14.03
   - (D) $14.17

---

6. 9,004
   −3,957
   - (A) 6,047
   - (B) 5,047
   - (C) 5,953
   - (D) 5,146

(See page 91 for answer key.)

CHAPTER 5

Multiplication

Multiplication is a new concept traditionally introduced in third grade, and a fair amount of time during the year is devoted to this area. By learning to apply these new concepts, students discover that they are able to tackle a whole array of new word problems that have been beyond their reach until this point. Many children perceive learning their "tables" as very grown up and usually embrace the task with enthusiasm. After the rigors of multistep subtraction, it can come as a welcome relief!

What Third Graders Should Know

Multiplication usually is introduced to students as repeated addition of the same numbers. Manipulatives such as base 10 blocks, counters, connecting cubes, beads, and so on can help students learn this new concept. They learn that when you have equal groups, you can add or you can multiply to find out how many there are in all. For example,

$$5 + 5 + 5 = 15$$

is repeated addition. Students are then encouraged to think of this as three groups of 5 that can be written as an equation horizontally or vertically. They learn that this is a convenient way to write down repeating facts that with large numbers could become very cumbersome.

Students usually have plenty of practice using manipulatives and are given the opportunity to see what a multiplication problem really looks like. They learn that when the order of the factors is changed, the product (answer) remains the same, although the groupings will be different.

Students also discover that the product of any number and 1 is always that number, and the product of any number and 0 is always 0. Third graders also learn that you always multiply factors in parentheses first, as illustrated below. Then the other factor is multiplied.

$$(2 \times 3) \times 4 = ?$$
$$6 \times 4 = 24$$

By the end of third grade, students usually are expected to know their 0 to 9 multiplication tables. Advanced math students may go on to learn their 10, 11, and 12 times tables. All sorts of strategies will be used in the classroom to make this process palatable: board games, flash cards, computer games, finding patterns in different tables, projects, and so on. Learning to apply the correct multiplication fact to solve word problems will be stressed, too.

Once their multiplication tables have been mastered, students can move on to multiplying two- and three-digit numbers by one digit. At first, they will use place-value charts and base 10 blocks to work through the process to find the product. Students also learn that multiplying three digits follows the same process. In both cases, your child needs to be very much aware that he must not add on regrouped tens or hundreds before he multiplies. This is a common error.

Estimating

The use of estimating is taught so that a rough idea of the product can be found quickly when there are two or more digits in one of the factors. The larger factor is rounded to the nearest ten or 100 and then multiplied.

What You and Your Child Can Do

Practice! Try to help your child keep up with the group as they proceed through the various times tables. This is where you can be most supportive. Practice will be provided in school, but most children will need extra practice at home, too.

Make Your Own Flash Cards. The use of the basic facts flash cards (discussed at some length in Chapter 2) can be applied to multiplication flash cards. Getting your child to make his own cards gives the whole process more meaning and a feeling of ownership. As your child is introduced to each new table, he can construct new cards and add them to the growing pile. Point out that as he goes along, he'll have fewer and fewer facts to learn because he will have already mastered them in the preceding tables. (For instance, by the time your child gets to his 9 times table, he will only have to learn 9 times 9.) This can be encouraging to your child because his early enthusiasm can begin to wane by the time he reaches his 7, 8, and 9 times tables.

Multiplication Games. If your child is reluctant, try musical multiplication math kits with cassettes or CDs as well as "Twist and Shout" devices, Wrap-up Rap, and the excellent game 24. These can be lots of fun and a nice change of pace from regular flash cards.

Use Counters. When multiplication is first introduced, use counters, beads, buttons, or beans and encourage your child to illustrate easy multiplication facts. You'll be able to see if he has fully grasped the concept. For instance, if you ask him to illustrate $5 \times 4 = 20$, he should have 5 groups with 4 counters in each group, making a total of 20 counters.

On the other hand, when you ask him to illustrate $4 \times 5 = 20$, he should have 4 groups with 5 counters in each group, also making a total of 20. However, each fact means and looks different, although the product is the same in both cases. You can practice this process many times to make sure your child fully understands what he is doing.

Domino Math. You also can use dominoes to make up multiplication facts. Have your child identify the number of dots on one side of a domino and write down the number and the multiplication sign. Finally, have him identify the number on the other side and solve the problem he has written down.

Math in Action. Have fun looking for things in the world around you that come in multiples, such as "bug math": If an insect has 6 legs, three insects have 18 legs ($3 \times 6 = 18$). Each human has 10 fingers, so five humans have 50 fingers ($5 \times 10 = 50$). Horses have 4 legs, so seven horses will have 28 legs ($7 \times 4 = 28$). Once you get going, your family probably will come up with most inventive and clever ideas, and your child will be learning at the same time.

Draw a Picture. When your child becomes stuck on one particular fact, it can be helpful to fix it in his mind by creating a picture. Suppose your child has problems with the multiplication fact $7 \times 8 = 56$ (which for some reason always seems to be a hard fact to remember). He can think of a creative way to illustrate it—perhaps 7 daisies with 8 petals on each flower so that there are 56 petals altogether. Maybe your child will think of 7 spider webs with 8 flies caught in each web so that there are 56 flies altogether. Underneath the illustration, he can write the multiplication fact and then descriptive sentences.

MULTIPLICATION

Multiplication Bingo. It's easy to make up game boards for Multiplication Bingo out of tagboard. Perhaps friends who come over to play or noncompetitive siblings would be willing to have a game. If none of these options are possible, your child could play against the clock.

Here's how to make the Bingo card:

1. Divide the boards up into 16 equal squares.
2. Write down products as illustrated below. You only fill in 8 of the squares because there needs to be space around the products so that they are clearly visible.
3. First make game boards with the products of 0 to 5 times tables displayed. Later you can move on to displaying products of 0 to 9 times tables. If you have a child who thrives on challenge, move on to include all the tables between 0 and 12. Then make up lists of appropriate multiplication facts to call out and use as a record to check covered products. The first person who covers all the products correctly with a card or counter wins the game.

21		32	
	63		72
56		28	
	42		49

Tips. There are some tips that you can pass on to your child that might be helpful. Note that the products of 5 show skip-counting, and the products of the 9 times table are always the sum of 9, except when the product is 0. When your child is having problems multiplying two or more digits, check to see that he is not adding on the regrouped tens or hundreds before he multiplies.

Multiplication War. Play the card game War with your child (remove face cards first), but instead of the traditional rules, each player throws a car and shouts out the product of the two cards. Whoever gives the correct answer first gets to keep the two cards.

What Tests May Ask

At the third-grade level, standardized tests will include questions on multiplying numerals and word problems in one- and two-digit numbers and may include some questions on estimating. Questions will be presented in both horizontal and vertical fashion. Students also may be asked to write a number sentence from an illustration.

Practice Skill: Multiplication

Directions: Read the following problems and select the correct answer.

Example:

$5 \times 6 =$ ___

- Ⓐ 25
- Ⓑ 28
- Ⓒ 30
- Ⓓ 36

Answer:

- Ⓒ 30

---

1 Write a number sentence for the following illustration.

00   00   00   00
00   00   00   00
00   00   00   00

- Ⓐ $6 \times 4 = 24$
- Ⓑ $4 + 6 = 10$
- Ⓒ $4 \times 6 = 25$
- Ⓓ $4 \times 6 = 28$

2 $7 \times 9 =$ ___
- Ⓐ 64
- Ⓑ 63
- Ⓒ 56
- Ⓓ 72

3 $\begin{array}{r}8\\ \times 4\\ \hline\end{array}$
- Ⓐ 24
- Ⓑ 40
- Ⓒ 34
- Ⓓ 32

4 $9 \times 80 =$ ___
- Ⓐ 7,200
- Ⓑ 810
- Ⓒ 640
- Ⓓ 720

5 Estimate: $6 \times 537 =$ ___.
- Ⓐ 3,222
- Ⓑ 3,600
- Ⓒ 3,000
- Ⓓ 300

6 $\begin{array}{r}83\\ \times\ 8\\ \hline\end{array}$
- Ⓐ 644
- Ⓑ 664
- Ⓒ 684
- Ⓓ 564

7 $9 \times 9 =$ ___
- Ⓐ 80
- Ⓑ 72
- Ⓒ 90
- Ⓓ 81

8 $0 \times 8 =$ ___
- Ⓐ 0
- Ⓑ 8
- Ⓒ 1
- Ⓓ 16

(See page 91 for answer key.)

CHAPTER 6

Division

In third grade, students begin to learn about division, the opposite mathematical operation to multiplication. The introduction of division frequently follows multiplication in the early spring of third grade.

What Third Graders Should Know

In third grade, students learn basic, simple division facts. As an introduction to division, students usually have the chance to use manipulatives such as counters, multilink cubes, buttons, beans, peanuts, and so on to discover the relationship between multiplication and division and to reinforce the idea of separating a group into equal groups.

Students are encouraged to think of the related multiplication facts to help them solve division problems. For instance, below are 15 X's arranged in three equal groups:

X X X X X   X X X X X   X X X X X

This could be described in two ways:

Multiplication: $3 \times 5 = 15$
Division: $15 \div 3 = 5$

Knowing multiplication and division fact families is important if students are going to be successful in recalling the related multiplication fact to solve a division fact. In third grade, students also learn certain rules:

- When you divide any number by 1, the quotient is that number.

  Example: $9 \div 1 = 9$

- When you divide 0 by any number, the quotient is always 0.

  Example: $24 \div 0 = 0$

- When you divide any number by itself, the quotient is always 1.

  Example: $12 \div 12 = 1$

Toward the end of the school year, when the students are comfortable with simple division, they move on to division with remainders. It is important that students remember that the remainder is *always less than the divisor*. Some third graders may be expected to divide three-digit numbers with remainders by the end of the school year.

Students also need to understand patterns in division. Here are examples.

$6 \div 2 = 3$	$8 \div 4 = 2$	$28 \div 7 = 4$	$30 \div 5 = 6$
$600 \div 2 = 300$	$80 \div 4 = 20$	$280 \div 7 = 40$	$300 \div 5 = 60$

With some practice, your child should be able to calculate these problems mentally. Students appreciate that usually the number of zeroes in the dividend tells you how many zeroes there will be in the quotient. However, this does not work when the dividend in the basic fact already has a zero in it.

What You and Your Child Can Do

Review Multiplication. By the time your child starts to study division, she should be feeling comfortable with her basic multiplication facts. This will give her the solid foundation that she will need to build on when she begins division. If this is not the case, you can be a great help in assisting her in her review of multiplication facts. Remember to approach this in a low-key manner so that your child doesn't think you are being in any way judgmental of her performance. Present your relationship as a partnership where you work together.

Flash Cards. From here you can move on to division flash cards and other appropriate learning tools to see if your child comprehends the concept behind division and its relationship with multiplication. Encourage her to think of the related multiplication fact and the missing factor to help her find the quotient.

Model It! Ask your child to model a division fact and explain what she is doing as she goes along. Give her 12 paper or plastic cups and a bag of beans, or muffin baking tins and beads would do just as well. Be creative in your thinking, and use whatever is handy. Ask your child to model a division fact, creating groups by placing beans in the cups or muffin tins, and explain what she is doing as she goes along. This technique is also useful to adopt when your child first begins dividing with remainders, too. She will clearly see how many beans are remaining.

How Many Ways? Here's a good game for a rainy day. Ask your child and a friend to see how many ways they can divide 24 beans—set the timer for a little competition:

24 ÷ 4 = 6   24 ÷ 6 = 4   24 ÷ 8 = 3   24 ÷ 3 = 8
24 ÷ 2 = 12   24 ÷ 12 = 2   24 ÷ 1 = 24   24 ÷ 24 = 1

Their results should be written down as division sentences. You could do the same thing using the numbers 12, 18, 30, 36, and 40, for example.

Check It. If your child is finding it difficult to work through division problems with remainders, check to see that she understands that the remainder always must be smaller than the divisor. An easy way for your child to check her division is to multiply the quotient and the divisor and then add the remainder to the product, which should give her the dividend of the problem if her calculations are correct. This is where a calculator can come in handy!

Make a Guide. It can be helpful to make a card with the order of procedures as a guide for your child as she works through multistep division problems. Many children become muddled and forget what to do next.

- Divide
- Multiply
- Subtract
- Compare
- Bring Down
- Start Over

To make the order of the steps easier for your child to remember, make up a nonsense sentence using the first letter of each word. Your child could write the words on a card and even illustrate it. The process will help fix the order in her mind as well as being lots of fun. Here is an example:

- Daddy
- Motored
- South
- Carrying
- Baby Dinosaurs
- Sleeping Obediently

Try to relate division to everyday life. Here are a few examples:

"If I give you 40 cents, how many nickels can you change them for?"

"How many dimes can I exchange for 80 cents?"

"How many dollar bills will you get at the bank for 500 cents?"

"If we take a vacation for 21 days, how many weeks will we be away?"

"Suppose we go away for 30 days. How many weeks will we then be away?"

"How many dozen egg cartons will you buy if you need 36 eggs?"

"If you gave me 29 socks to wash, how many pairs of socks will there be? Will there be any spare socks left over?"

Division Bingo. You may want to make or buy a Division Bingo game so that your child can practice her division facts. Instructions in the preceding chapter for making a Multiplication Bingo game can be adapted easily to division. Other games and aids referred to in the preceding chapter have similar counterparts addressing division and can be purchased at an educational store. Look for the *24 Game Primer, Factors Multiply Divide,* and the game *Division Down Under.*

What Tests May Ask

Division questions on standardized tests in third grade appear both in isolation and as word problems. Questions will be presented horizontally, with the division sign (÷), and with the division bar. In third grade, tests present division facts with and without remainders.

Practice Skill: Division

Directions: Complete each problem.

Example:

$25 \div 5 =$ ___
- Ⓐ 105
- Ⓑ 5
- Ⓒ 25
- Ⓓ 20

Answer:
- Ⓑ 5

---

1 $12 \div 4 =$ ___
- Ⓐ 3
- Ⓑ 8
- Ⓒ 2
- Ⓓ not given

---

2 $6 \div 2 =$ ___
- Ⓐ 6
- Ⓑ 3
- Ⓒ 4
- Ⓓ 12

---

3 $9 \div$ ___ $= 3$
- Ⓐ 5
- Ⓑ 3
- Ⓒ 2
- Ⓓ 9

---

4 $16 \div$ ___ $= 2$
- Ⓐ 8
- Ⓑ 6
- Ⓒ 2
- Ⓓ 5

---

5 $10 \div$ ___ $= 5$
- Ⓐ 1
- Ⓑ 2
- Ⓒ 5
- Ⓓ 15

(See page 91 for answer key.)

Practice Skill: Division with Remainders

Directions: Complete each problem.

Example:

26 ÷ 5 = ___

- Ⓐ 105
- Ⓑ 5 r 1
- Ⓒ 4 r 5
- Ⓓ 5 r 2

Answer:

- Ⓑ 5 r 1

---

6 ___ ÷ 10 = 2 r 2

- Ⓐ 30
- Ⓑ 22
- Ⓒ 40
- Ⓓ 5

---

9 9 ÷ 2 = ___

- Ⓐ 4 r 1
- Ⓑ 4 r 2
- Ⓒ 4
- Ⓓ 4 r 3

---

8 5) 22

- Ⓐ 5 r 2
- Ⓑ 2 r 2
- Ⓒ 10
- Ⓓ 4 r 2

---

9 2) 21

- Ⓐ 10 r 1
- Ⓑ 4 r 1
- Ⓒ 8
- Ⓓ 5 r 1

---

10 6) 15

- Ⓐ 3
- Ⓑ 2 r 3
- Ⓒ 2 r 2
- Ⓓ 6

(See page 91 for answer key.)

CHAPTER 7

Fractions and Decimals

Third graders begin to learn about fractions and decimals toward the end of the school year, when they have developed math skills that will give them a better understanding of these more challenging concepts. Decimals naturally follow fractions in this grade and are introduced formally for the first time.

Fractions

By third grade, most students will be able to use simple fractions to describe things, such as "half an apple" or "a quarter of the class," during their everyday conversations. Usually, the study of fractions in third grade is introduced with plenty of hands-on activities and manipulatives. If math textbooks are used, they will have attractive graphics for the children to look at when the various concepts are introduced.

What Third Graders Should Know

The introduction of fractions into the curriculum presents students with a different way to understand numbers. They now need to take a whole and split it into parts. Students will have been exposed to simple fractions in their everyday lives as well as learning about them in lower grades. Third graders need to understand what a fraction looks like and to be familiar with the relationship between basic fractions. They will learn what fractions are, the correct vocabulary, and that fractions can be a part of a set or a part of a whole. By the end of third grade, students will be able to compare and order fractions and identify equivalent fractions.

First, students will review parts of a whole when the whole is divided into equal parts in different ways and written as a fraction. They will be expected to identify and name as a fraction a particular part or parts of the whole. They learn that the number above the line in a fraction is called the *numerator* and tells how many parts of the whole are being referred to and that the number below the line is called the *denominator* and tells how many parts there are altogether in the whole. Students learn to identify parts of a group as a fraction. More advanced students will learn that they can divide to find the fractional part of a group.

For instance, to discover what a third of 9 hearts would be, the student would divide the 9 hearts into 3 equal groups ($9 \div 3 = 3$). There will be 3 hearts in each group.

Students will then be able to move on to find complex fractional parts of a group. One-ninth of 72, for instance, is 8 ($72 \div 9 = 8$). Once they know this, students can calculate what four-ninths of 72 would be ($4 \times 8 = 32$). Students usually enjoy applying what they have learned in division to another section of math and begin to see how to make use of this skill once they have become proficient in the process.

In third grade, your child will be expected to understand *equivalent fractions,* which can be a challenging concept for some children. The more hands-on activities they are exposed to, the more readily they can grasp the new concept. Students are also taught to compare fractions with the "greater than" sign (>), the "less than" sign (<), and the "equals" sign (=). They learn to appreciate that when two fractions have the same denominator, the greater fraction is the one with the greater numerator. And when two fractions have numerators that are the same, the one with the lesser denominator is the greater fraction because the size of the parts will be greater.

In third grade your child also will learn about *mixed numbers* (a number that has a whole number and a fraction, for instance $2\frac{1}{2}$). Students should be able to write fractions for parts and wholes. They should be able to compare fractions, and add and subtract fractions with like denominators.

What You and Your Child Can Do

Math in Action. You'll be surprised how often fractions come up in the course of a child's day. Let your child help divide pizzas, cakes, apples, oranges, bars of chocolate, and so on into equal parts. This can be an excellent way to reinforce in a visual manner the concept of what fraction each part is of a whole.

Cook Up Fractions. Cooking and eating present many good ways to work with fractions. As you cook, look for ways to share fractions with your child. Have him measure out a half cup of sugar. Ask which ingredient is greater—a half cup of sugar or a quarter cup of oil.

Math Around the House. You can find examples of fractions all around the house if you only look. Have your child search for things that are divided into equal parts and then draw them—for example, sliding doors or window panes. Have your child color a portion of the picture and then label the fraction it represents—for example, coloring in half a sliding glass door would be an example of $\frac{1}{2}$. Then your child can sort the pictures and figure out which fraction has the most examples.

Math Software. There are many wonderful software programs that teach math to children in third grade using great graphics and fun games. Here are only a few of the many possibilities:

- *Schoolhouse Rock 3rd and 4th Grade Essentials* (Creative Wonders)
- *Reader Rabbit's Math Ages 6–9* (The Learning Company)
- *Star Wars Math: Jabba's Game Galaxy* (Lucas Learning)
- *Turbo Math Facts 3.0* (Nordic Software)
- *Brain Quest Third Grade* (IBM)
- *Knowledge Quest Math* (CBE Services)
- *Math Blaster Age 8–9* (Knowledge Adventure)

What Tests May Ask

As a way of testing the extent to which your third grader has understood math concepts, many types of standardized tests will measure how well your child can add and subtract fractions. Most standardized tests will supply several possible answers to a question and ask your child to choose the correct answer. Many tests also include a "not given" or "none of the above" choice. Be sure your child understands what the choice means.

FRACTIONS AND DECIMALS

Practice Skill: Fractions

Directions: Choose the correct answer for the following problems.

Example:

$1/3 + 1/3 =$ ___

- Ⓐ $1/3$
- Ⓑ $2/3$
- Ⓒ $3/3$
- Ⓓ none of the above

Answer:

- Ⓑ $2/3$

---

1 $1/5 + 2/5 =$ ___
- Ⓐ $1/5$
- Ⓑ $2/5$
- Ⓒ $3/5$
- Ⓓ $4/5$

2 $9/10 - 1/10 =$ ___
- Ⓐ $10/10$
- Ⓑ $8/10$
- Ⓒ $7/10$
- Ⓓ $6/10$

3 $1/8$ of 56
- Ⓐ 7
- Ⓑ 6
- Ⓒ 9
- Ⓓ 8

4 $4/8$ ___ $1/2$
- Ⓐ =
- Ⓑ <
- Ⓒ >
- Ⓓ $4/8$

5 $2/16 + 8/16 =$ ___
- Ⓐ $6/16$
- Ⓑ $10/16$
- Ⓒ $8/16$
- Ⓓ $2/16$

6 Choose the correct order from smallest to largest in the following fractions.
- Ⓐ $1/4, 1/3, 1/2$
- Ⓑ $1/3, 1/2, 1/4$
- Ⓒ $1/3, 1/4, 1/2$
- Ⓓ none of the above

(See page 91 for answer key.)

Decimals

Third-grade students should be able to write decimals for $1/2$ and $1/4$, and compare fractions and decimals. Decimals may seem difficult to a third grader, but there are many ways you can show how we all use decimals in everyday life. Your child has already used decimals if he's used money, had his temperature taken, checked a batting average, worked with a calculator, or helped you pump gas. While formal study of decimals really begins in fourth grade, many third graders have already reviewed decimals as they studied place value and as they added and subtracted money values.

What Third Graders Should Know

In third grade your child will practice adding and subtracting numbers involving decimals, including money problems, but most children won't get into comparing or ordering decimals.

What You and Your Child Can Do

Encourage your child's interest in and knowledge of decimals by talking about those you come across in your daily life. Money is the easiest way for your child to think about decimals.

Make Change. Have your child practice making change. Have him count up from the cost of an item beginning with the smallest coins first. The next time you go to the store, let your child pay and have him count the change.

Decimal Cards. If your child needs some practice in decimals, try making your own flash cards. Write fractions and decimals on 3 × 5 inch cards, and see how many your child can match in 1 minute.

What Tests May Ask

Standardized tests will assess how well your child understands decimals in a variety of ways. Some questions will present a decimal and ask your child to identify tenths or hundredths place, or present a number in long form and ask for the number name.

Other questions may present a shaded figure and ask your child to identify the decimal that represents the shaded portion. Money questions may also be included here.

Practice Skill: Decimals

Directions: Solve each problem below.

Example:

In the number 40.53, what number is in the *tenths* place?

Ⓐ 0
Ⓑ 5
Ⓒ 4
Ⓓ 2

Answer:

Ⓑ 5

---

7 For the number 3.7, what number is in the *tenths* place?

Ⓐ 4
Ⓑ 3
Ⓒ 7
Ⓓ 6

---

8 What is the number name for six hundred thirty-four and two-tenths?

Ⓐ 634.029
Ⓑ 643.2
Ⓒ 634.29
Ⓓ none of the above

---

9 Write the fraction and the decimal for the shaded area in the figure below.

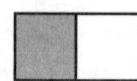

Ⓐ ½ or .5
Ⓑ ⅓ or .1
Ⓒ ⁴⁄₁₀ or .04
Ⓓ none of the above

FRACTIONS AND DECIMALS

10 Add $6.00 and $3.50.
- Ⓐ $6.68
- Ⓑ About $7.00
- Ⓒ $6.685
- Ⓓ none of the above

11 You bought a doll at a yard sale for $1.50. You gave the cashier a $5 bill. How much change will you receive?
- Ⓐ $4.50
- Ⓑ About $1.00
- Ⓒ $3.50
- Ⓓ none of the above

12 Solve the problem: 5.3 + 2.1 = ___.
- Ⓐ 3.2
- Ⓑ 7.2
- Ⓒ 3.4
- Ⓓ 7.4

(See page 91 for answer key.)

CHAPTER 8

Place Value, Number Sense, and Money

During the first weeks of the new school year, students review the place values and order of numbers up to one thousand. They then quickly move on to acquiring a more sophisticated sense of our number system through various activities involving

- Ordinal numbers
- Place value up to hundreds of thousands
- Rounding numbers to tens and hundreds
- Comparing, ordering, reading, and writing larger numbers

What Third Graders Should Know

Children usually are intrigued by large numbers and are eager to learn how to read and write millions, although this is an area that is not usually addressed in third-grade math books or in official testing.

Students also are encouraged to think of the countless ways we use numbers to help us in our daily lives. Often the fascinating historical background of numbers and money is explored and discussed. Students review the various coins and bills so that they are able to recognize them without hesitation. They become competent at counting money and giving change through various cooperative hands-on activities with their classmates. Throughout the year, they will continue to build on these skills.

Students often use base 10 blocks and place-value mats to model larger numbers. They should be able to explain how they know the value of a digit by its position and be able to model a number to prove it. For instance in the number 5,784, the value of the digit 5 is 5 thousands, 7 is 7 hundreds, 8 is 8 tens, and 4 is 4 ones. Students also should be able to both interpret and record the various ways numbers can be presented. Below is an example of the different ways a number can be recorded:

- 6,483 (the *standard form* of the number)
- 6 thousands, 4 hundreds, 8 tens, 3 ones (the *place-value name* for the number)
- six thousand, four hundred eighty-three (the *word name* for the number) (Note that there is a comma after the thousand.)
- 6,000 + 400 + 80 + 3 (the *expanded form* of the number)

Missing Numbers

Students will review counting ones, tens, and hundreds and practice using patterns to find *missing numbers*. Examples include

17, 19, ___, 23, ___, ___, ___ (counting odd numbers)

80, 90, ___, 110, ___, ___ (counting by tens)

472, 473, ___, 475, ___, ___ (counting by ones)

13,400; ___; 13,600; ___; 13,800, ___ (counting by hundreds)

Students will learn to write the numbers that come just *before* and just *after* larger numbers. Example: 639 (638, 640).

Students also will become proficient at recording numbers that *come between* certain numbers. Example: 4,999 and 5,002 (5,000, 5,001). They also will learn to order numbers efficiently from *greatest* to *least*, for example, 4,778, 3,887, 4,878, 3,787 (4,878, 4,778 3,887 3,787) and from *least* to *greatest,* for example, $5,632, $3,627, $5,600, $5,621 ($3,627, $5,600, $5,621, $5,632).

When comparing two numbers, the symbols < and > are often used. The symbol > means "is greater than" (635 > 625). The open end of the symbol is directed toward the larger number. Sometimes this is explained as a crocodile opening its jaws to gobble up the larger number. This visual picture often helps children who have difficulties accurately distinguishing between these symbols. The symbol < means "is less than" (415,089 < 415,198). The pointed end of the symbol is directed toward the lesser number.

When students are ordering numbers, they are often encouraged to line up the numbers vertically and then compare the first digits of the numbers, then the second digits of the numbers, and so on. Frequently, *number lines* (a line that shows numbers in order) are used to help children find number patterns or arrange numbers in order. For example:

Ordinal Numbers

Students learn how to use and write *ordinal numbers* correctly, a concept they will already have been exposed to in earlier grades An ordinal number shows order or position, such as *third, twenty-ninth,* and *forty-second*. Students are encouraged to think of various situations where ordinal numbers are used, for instance, in the order of the days in each month, the position of runners in a marathon race, the position of letters in the alphabet, and so on.

Students also should understand the different spellings at the ends of the numbers to create ordinal numbers. Many end with *th,* such as fourth, fifth, sixth, eighty-seventh, and three-hundredth. The endings *st, nd,* and *rd* are added to first, second, third, and other numbers with the same ending. In third grade, students are expected to write the ordinal numbers in words.

Rounding

Students learn to *round* numbers to the nearest ten and then to the nearest hundred. The students learn that the term *to round* means "about how many," not "exactly how many."

For example, the number 42 is between the two tens—40 and 50. It will *round down* to the closest ten, which is 40. Any two-digit number ending with the digit 4 or under *rounds down* to the nearest ten. The number 48, on the other hand, will *round up* to the closest ten, which is 50. Any two-digit number ending with a 5 or above *rounds up* to the next ten automatically. Therefore, 35 will *round up* to 40. For example:

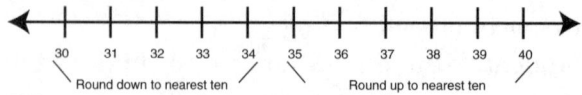

Rounding to the nearest hundred follows the same principal. The number 549 is between the hundreds 500 and 600. Because it is less than 550, it will *round down* to 500. All three-digit numbers ending with 50 or above automatically *round up* to the next hundred. For instance, 782 *rounds up* to 800.

Students are also taught how to round money to the nearest dollar. If the cents part is 50¢ or more, you *round up* to the next dollar amount. If

PLACE VALUE, NUMBER SENSE, AND MONEY

the cents part is 49¢ or less, you *round down*. For instance, $8.69 *rounds up* to $9.00, and $8.21 *rounds down* to $8.00. Some students can find rounding confusing, particularly when they are asked to round a three-digit number to the nearest *ten*. For instance, 724 rounded to the nearest ten would be 720. Students need to understand they are asked to round to the nearest *ten*, not hundred.

By third grade, most students will have had opportunities to handle money both in and out of school and should be able to recognize and name the various coins. However, as a rule, children don't have as many opportunities these days to handle coins and bills in realistic situations as they might have done in years gone by. They often need a review of values and require plenty of hands-on experiences counting coins and making change with play money.

Students should remember the strategy they were taught in second grade to count from the greatest to the least, first counting the largest bills through to the $1 bills and then moving on to half dollars, quarters, dimes, nickels, and lastly pennies.

Students learn to appreciate that when you make change, it is the opposite process from counting money. You always start by counting the smallest denomination of money and gradually working up to the largest.

What You and Your Child Can Do

There are many ways you can engage your child's interest in numbers that are informal and fun. When you visit the children's section of your local library, look for books about numbers. The history of numbers and money can be quite fascinating. This interesting background information is also easily accessible on the Internet.

Math in Action. There are many ways to involve your child in everyday math. Try counting scores in sports; class attendances; the populations of cities, states, countries, and continents; money; miles; and ages. *Measure* the weights of people and parcels; quantities for recipes; the heights of people, buildings, trees, and mountains; shoe and clothing sizes; the lengths of rooms, draperies, rivers, and football fields; time; and temperature. *Identify numbers* such as a license plate, bank account, Social Security Number, telephone numbers, and zip codes.

Newspaper Find. Encourage your child to look in a newspaper for a number of days and locate large numbers. Cut them out and then arrange them from the least to the greatest. Then ask her to record the greatest number in standard, place-value, word, and expanded forms. If your child finds this challenging, ask her to find a number she would feel more comfortable naming. From this activity you will be able to gauge your child's understanding of place values.

If your child has a sophisticated appreciation of numbers, she will be able to handle numbers into the millions. For instance, the standard form for the number 9,567,204 in the expanded number form would be

9,000,000 + 500,000 + 60,000 + 7,000 + 200 + 4

As you can see, although there is a zero in the tens place in the standard form, it is left out in the expanded number. Children by third grade should be aware that the hundreds are separated from the thousands by a comma, and some will quickly pick up that hundreds of thousands are separated from the millions also by a comma. Millions are not officially introduced in most third-grade curriculums, but the curious child who is fascinated by numbers will enjoy using them. The bigger the number, the better!

Place-Value Chart. If your child seems unsure of herself, you may want to make cards with various numbers on them and ask her the values of various digits. If this is still challenging, you may want to make a place-value chart like the one below for your child to record numbers as you give them to her. This will help identify each digit's value. Gradually introduce larger numbers as the child's confidence grows. Remind her that she should always start on the right with the ones. For the number 156,789:

Hundreds of Thousands	Tens of Thousands	Thousands	Hundreds	Tens	Ones
1	5	6,	7	8	9

Real Money. Give your child as many opportunities as possible to handle real money. Allowances are always a good idea to help teach money facts, but if your child doesn't get an allowance, you can still create experiences where she handles coins and bills and becomes comfortable counting money and giving change. Saving up pocket money for a special reason can be a very worthwhile experience for children. They will naturally be very much aware of how much they have and how much more they need to save for a special event or toy.

Coin Collections. If your child finds it difficult to identify the individual coins, you can help by taking the time to examine the coins carefully with her. If you use a magnifying glass, it can be even more fun because the child will notice the small details. Encyclopedias usually have a list and pictures of the Presidents with their dates that would be useful to have at hand. Examine each coin carefully, looking at each President. Tell your child to look at the hair styles and dress. Ask her if the coins show recent presidents or ones from the distant past. This can lead to lively discussions. Once the President is identified, the child can look up her dates, and you can talk a little about why this particular President is significant. Looking at the flip side of the coin is also interesting. Children always enjoy seeing if they can find Lincoln's statue in his memorial and learning about Monticello, the house Jefferson designed and built in Virginia. You will find after this activity that the coins will have their own separate identities in your child's mind.

What Tests May Ask

Only a page or two of most standardized tests are devoted to money, including questions that typically ask students to identify amounts of money from pictures of coins and bills, to choose an alternate way to make a given amount, and to round dollar amounts. There may be some word problems and one or two questions about making change. Some tabulation may need to be done on scratch paper and then transferred to the test page.

Other questions will require your child to demonstrate understanding of ordinal position, rounding up and down to the nearest ten or hundred, and identifying number patterns by choosing a missing number to complete a pattern.

Practice Skill: Place Value, Number Sense, and Money

Directions: Read the following problems and select the correct answer.

1. Choose the correct position of the letter *i* in the alphabet.
    - Ⓐ eleventh
    - Ⓑ tenth
    - Ⓒ ninth
    - Ⓓ eighth

PLACE VALUE, NUMBER SENSE, AND MONEY

2 What is the least whole number that rounds to 900?

- Ⓐ 899
- Ⓑ 850
- Ⓒ 950
- Ⓓ 849

3 Choose the correct group of missing numbers.

325, 425, ___, ___, 725, ___, 925, ___

- Ⓐ 620, 725, 850, 950
- Ⓑ 550, 625, 850, 1,025
- Ⓒ 525, 625, 825, 1,025
- Ⓓ 225, 125, 1,025, 1,250

4 Choose the correct way of recording the number 28,059 in expanded form.

- Ⓐ 20,000 + 8,000 + 50 + 9
- Ⓑ 28,000 + 800 + 59
- Ⓒ 2,000 + 800 + 50 + 9
- Ⓓ 20,000 + 8,000 + 500 + 90

5 Choose the numbers that come before and after 6,000.

- Ⓐ 5,999 and 6,001
- Ⓑ 5,900 and 6,100
- Ⓒ 5,901 and 6,010
- Ⓓ 5,990 and 6,110

6 Count the money below and choose the correct value.

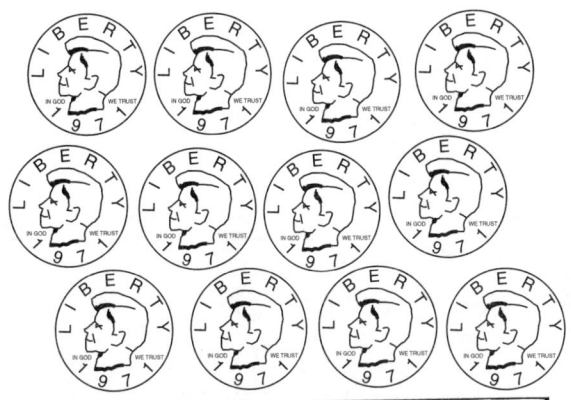

- Ⓐ $16.94
- Ⓑ $15.84
- Ⓒ $15.89
- Ⓓ $15.94

7 Round $8.48 to the nearest dollar and then choose the correct answer.

- Ⓐ $9.00
- Ⓑ $8.00
- Ⓒ $8.50
- Ⓓ $8.40

8 You buy a small notebook for $1.57. You give the sales clerk a $5 bill. Choose the correct amount of change you will receive.

- Ⓐ $3.53
- Ⓑ $2.43
- Ⓒ $3.44
- Ⓓ $3.43

(See page 91 for answer key.)

CHAPTER 9

Geometry

These days children are introduced to the concept of geometry very early in their school career, usually through numerous hands-on activities involving manipulatives and visual images as well as everyday objects. Most students love geometry and often say that it's their favorite math unit. This is particularly true for the very visual child, who often shines in this area. Geometry involves lots of hands-on activities with concrete objects as students are encouraged to look at their environment in a new way. They will be encouraged to make connections between what they observe and what they are learning.

Students usually will have no difficulties recognizing the *two-dimensional figures* (sometimes referred to as *plane figures*), such as squares, rectangles, triangles, and circles. *Three-dimensional figures* may be more challenging. Very often the geometry unit is introduced with a set of wooden geometric three-dimensional figures. A can, an orange, a tissue box, an ice cream cone, a pair of dice—all these are just a few examples of everyday three-dimensional figures. Your child will be encouraged to see the attributes that various figures have in common, noticing which figures have flat or curved faces, straight or curved edges, no edges, corners, or no corners. They may be expected to count the various characteristics and tabulate their findings on a chart.

Geometric figures can be *open* or *closed,* and your child will learn how to tell the difference between them. *Polygons* (closed figures with straight sides) are also introduced in third grade. Your child will learn how to distinguish between the different figures and will be expected to learn their names and know how many sides they each have. Often students will work with a partner and take turns to create and name polygons using a geoboard or dot paper.

Lines and Angles. Students also learn about *lines, line segments, rays,* and *angles* in a formal manner for the first time in third grade. Some students find it quite challenging to differentiate between the various types of lines and need lots of practice. A *line segment* is part of a line; it is straight, with two end points. The sides making up squares, rectangles, and triangles are all line segments. This is a line segment:

A *line* is straight and has no end points but goes on forever in both directions. This is a line:

A *ray* is part of a line. It has one end point and goes on forever in one direction. This is a ray:

An *angle* is formed when two rays or line segments come together at an end point. All right angles are the same size. The corner of an index card, a book, and a window frame are perfect examples of right angles because they have square corners. Third graders will be encouraged to look around the classroom and home to find their own examples of each kind of angle. Students probably will have practice forming their own angles and deciding what type they make either with their hands or with a homemade device with strips of card and a brass fastener. These are angles:

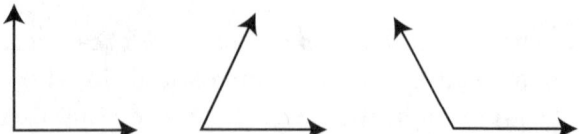

Patterns. Students have already had some experience with *patterns* when they come to third grade. When presented with a pattern problem, students have learned to look very carefully to discover the order in which the figures have been arranged so that they can continue the pattern. For instance, with the pattern

=**ooo=**ooo=**

a child can quickly see the pattern. With numbers, it can be more challenging. In the case of 1, 2, 4, 8, 16, __, __, __, __, the pattern might not be so obvious. The student needs to study the numbers carefully to see the relationships and find the rule. In this case, the numbers double each time, so they continue 32, 64, 128, 256, and so on.

Congruent Figures. By third grade, students should be familiar with *congruent figures*—figures that have the same size and shape. Congruent figures will match perfectly if they are placed on top of each other.

Symmetry. A figure has *symmetry* if it can be folded along a line (the *line of symmetry*) so that the parts match exactly. Students also discover that some figures such as squares, rectangles, and circles, have more than one line of symmetry. Others, such as a triangle with different side lengths, do not.

What Third Graders Should Know

During third grade, students gain a more sophisticated appreciation of two- and three-dimensional shapes as they learn more about polygons, lines, line segments, rays, and angles. Your child will learn to identify more complex congruent figures and to move two-dimensional shapes by sliding, flipping, and turning them. In addition, your child should be able to identify a pyramid, sphere, cube, cone, cylinder, and rectangular prism. Third graders learn to distinguish lines of symmetry from other lines and to draw their own lines of symmetry on a symmetrical figure.

What You and Your Child Can Do

As you can see, there are many geometric connections you can make for your child both at home and in your neighborhood. Looking at houses and public buildings, you'll be surprised at the number of two- and three-dimensional figures you can pick out. You'll also see that we are surrounded by examples of angles, line segments, and rays. Once your child has some grasp of these figures, you can go for a stroll and see how many you both can spot and name.

Cubism. The artists who invented Cubism at the turn of the twentieth century used geometric shapes in their paintings and sculptures. Check out a book of modern paintings and see if you can find any examples to show your child.

Sense It. If your child has trouble distinguishing among *three-dimensional* figures, try this game. Get a bag and gather up various objects such as a can of soup, a tennis ball, a roll of toilet paper, a tissue box, a cereal box, a candle, a kaleidoscope, two dice, a crayon box, a pingpong ball, and so on. Let your child reach into the bag, choose an object, feel its surfaces, and then name it. The child can then pull the object out of the bag and see if he is correct. If he is correct, you can ask him how many surfaces, how many edges, and how many corners the figure has. He also could name the related two-dimensional figure, for instance, a sphere with a circle, a rectangular prism with a rectangle, and so on. Other members of the family could be encouraged to join in the game.

Model It. It can be lots of fun to build *two-dimensional polygons* out of straws and modeling clay and then move on to the more challenging three-dimensional figures. The straws are attached to each other by rolling the clay into small balls and gradually building them into a figure. Each straw and attached clay balls represents a line segment, and each corner created by attaching another straw is an angle. Your child should name and label each model he makes. Another way to create polygons would be to glue tooth picks or craft sticks together.

Geoboards. You can buy commercial geoboards from an educational store for a reasonable price. This is an excellent way to create two-dimensional figures. Children always enjoy working with them.

Alphabet Symmetry. You can use capital letters to illustrate the concept of symmetry. Have your child print the letter B—and then print it backward. Does it look the same? Of course not! Now have your child print the letter A. A is different—because it's symmetrical; both sides look the same, not different. Go through the alphabet making a list of the letters that are symmetrical (look the same on both sides) and those which aren't. For instance, H, M, O, and T are symmetrical, but D, C, J, and R are not.

Alphabet Angles. As long as you're searching the alphabet, ask your child to see how many angles each letter has. Are they right angles, less than right angles, or greater than right angles? You also can discuss the number of line segments a letter might have. For instance, the letter N has three line segments.

Symmetrical Bugs. Insects are fascinating to children of this age and lend themselves well to drawings of symmetry. You can photocopy diagrams of insects, divide them symmetrically, cut around them, attach them to a clean piece of paper with matte plastic tape, and then copy them. Your child will have a wonderful time copying the other side of the insects and at the same time learn the true meaning of symmetry. Or have your child cut objects out of magazines, divide them symmetrically, glue them onto blank paper, and then draw the other, unsymmetrical part.

Concentration. There are a lot of geometric terms to learn in third grade. One way to help your child learn these terms is to draw on note cards the various two-dimensional, three-dimensional, and polygon figures—plus the various types of lines and angles. Your drawings don't have to be perfect, just recognizable! For each card there should be a matching card with the correct geometric term printed on it. Your child then needs to match each pair up.

Commercial Geometric Shapes. Head to a good educational store where you can buy wooden three-dimensional geometric figures, sets of tangrams to create many geometric figures, and activity kits that can be used to show congruence and patterns, all at reasonable prices. If the store doesn't have a particular item in stock, ask the proprietor if there is a catalogue from which you can order.

What Tests May Ask

Standardized tests will ask students to identify certain shapes, give definitions of geometric terms, and select matching shapes. Students may be asked to find the one correct answer in a group of incorrect ones or to choose the incorrect response in a list of correct answers. There may be a "none of the above" statement as well.

Practice Skill: Geometry

Directions: Read the following problems and choose the correct answer.

Example:

What kind of an angle do the hands of a clock make at 3:00?

- Ⓐ a right angle
- Ⓑ less than a right angle
- Ⓒ greater than a right angle
- Ⓓ none of the above

Answer:

- Ⓐ a right angle

1 Choose the cylinder from among the shapes pictured below.

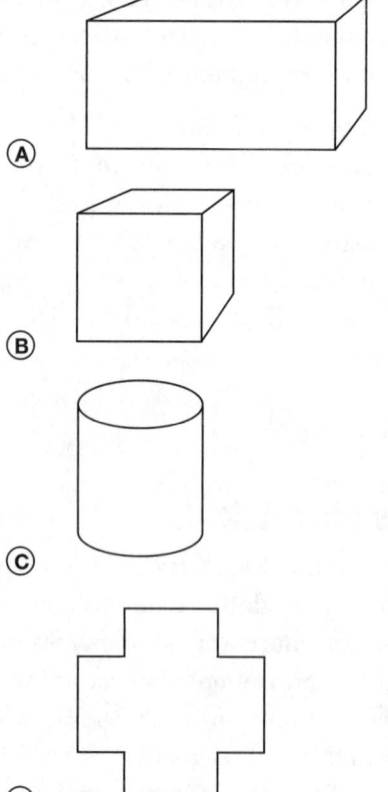

2 How many sides does the figure below have?

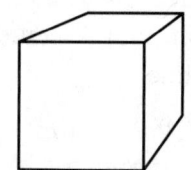

- Ⓐ 3
- Ⓑ 4
- Ⓒ 6
- Ⓓ 5

3 Which one of these figures is *not* a polygon?

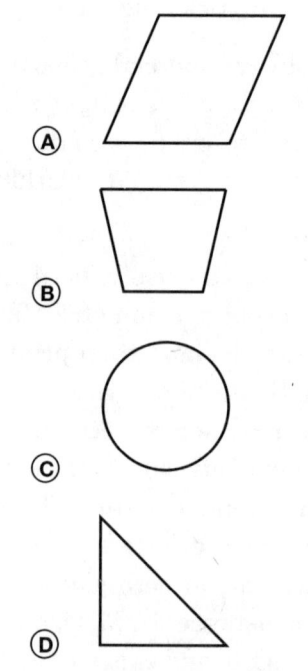

4 This figure is a what?

- Ⓐ line segment
- Ⓑ line
- Ⓒ ray
- Ⓓ angle

GEOMETRY

5 Complete the following pattern.

* & ** & *** && * & ** & ***

- Ⓐ *
- Ⓑ **
- Ⓒ &
- Ⓓ &&

6 Which figure below shows a correct line of symmetry?

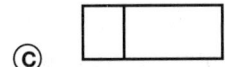
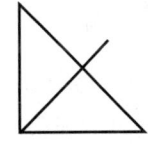

7 A door is 7 feet long and 3 feet wide. What is the perimeter of the door?

- Ⓐ 17 feet
- Ⓑ 20 feet
- Ⓒ 21 feet
- Ⓓ 24 feet

(See page 91 for answer key.)

Perimeter, Area, and Volume

Although the concepts of perimeter and area were introduced in second grade; now students build on this knowledge to tackle more complicated problems. They are also introduced to volume for the first time.

Most students easily understand that the distance around a closed shape or object is called the *perimeter*. They will be given a variety of hands-on experiences calculating the perimeters of different shapes using both metric and linear methods.

It will become apparent to your child that it's much easier to find the perimeter of a shape if it has straight sides, and that if a shape is square, only one side must be measured because the other three will be equal. By the time students are in third grade, they should feel comfortable measuring in inches and feet as well as centimeters and meters.

To understand *area,* children need plenty of practical experiences. Frequently, this topic is introduced using square plastic tiles, centimeter graph paper, the squares on a geoboard, magazine pictures of rooms where the floors are covered with square tiles, or better still, an area in the school where the floors are covered with square tiles. Students are then encouraged to count all the squares to see how many were needed to cover the particular area under discussion.

At first, students will be expected to calculate areas of squares and rectangles by counting the number of square units making up the shape. Later, students learn that multiplication can be a much quicker method to find the area of a regular shape than counting each square unit.

Volume is the number of cubic units that fit inside a three-dimensional figure. To help students grasp this new concept, they may be shown standard containers used to measure liquids and asked to arrange them according to the amount of liquid they hold from least to greatest (a cup, a pint, a quart, a gallon). From similar examples, students will grasp that the larger the three-dimensional figure, the more space there is inside it and that this space is called the *volume* of a figure. This is a concept that can be quite challenging for some students to grasp fully without plenty of hands-on experience.

Often after the initial introduction to volume a teacher will demonstrate the concept by building regular three-dimensional figures with connecting plastic cubes. Students will have plenty of opportunities to work with connecting cubes to create "regular" and "irregular" three-dimensional figures and calculate their volume, as well as solving written problems where they will have diagrams to work from.

What You and Your Child Can Do

While your child is studying perimeter, area, and volume, you can generate an interesting discussion on applying the measurements to everyday life.

Everyday Perimeter. Why might it be important to know perimeter? For example, perimeter is important if you need to build an electric barrier to keep your dogs at home, to determine the property line around your house, or to measure around the inside of a window frame for a new piece of glass.

Everyday Area. Ask your child what situations would require knowing the area of a space. For instance, workers might need to calculate the area of a floor when they are installing wall-to-wall carpets or laying tile floors. A painter needs to know the area of the walls to be painted so that he or she can calculate the amount of paint needed, and a surveyor should know the area of a plot of land when it is to be sold.

Everyday Volume. It might be more difficult for a third grader to come up with examples of the application of volume. For example, a garden center sells mulch by the cubic yard, and the effectiveness of air conditioners are measured by the cubic feet of air they can control. Bring up these topics casually, and don't belabor them; just making the connections plants the seed! Usually you can judge when your child gets bored.

Measure It. Finding the *area* of a hand can be a fun activity. Have your child place his hand (fingers together) on 1-inch graph paper and trace around it. (You may need to point out that his hand starts at the wrist bone.) Then color each complete square one color, and each partial square another. Next, have your child count up the whole squares and record them. Then count the partial squares as half squares and record them, too. Finally, have your child add up all the squares and find the area of his hand in square inches. The child could then measure the areas of the hands of other family members and compare them. Another alternative is finding the area of feet!

Estimate Area. If your child is having trouble grasping the concept of area, you might find this simple project helpful. Explain that the area of an object is the number of square units that will cover it. What you'll need:

- A number of rectangular objects such as a book, a cassette tape, and a notecard
- One-inch colored tiles or one-inch paper squares, notecards, and a pencil

Now, here's what to do:

1. Ask your child to estimate the number of tiles or paper squares he thinks it will take to cover a book.
2. Record his findings.
3. Ask him to cover the book with rows of tiles or squares and count them. This will give him the approximate area of the book in square inches.
4. Record this on the card.
5. Compare his results with his estimate.

GEOMETRY

As your child proceeds with estimating, measuring, and recording different objects, he probably will find that estimating becomes more accurate.

Shape Change. On centimeter graph paper, have your child draw three different shapes with a 12-centimeter *perimeter*. Find the area of each. Record the perimeter and area within each shape. Your child will see that the area can change when the configuration of the perimeter changes.

Build a Cube. To explore *volume,* get some connecting plastic cubes at an educational store—or use sugar cubes. Give your child 8 cubes, and let him build a rectangular prism using all the cubes. He should realize that the volume of the structure he has built is 8 cubic units. (If the edges of the cube are exactly an inch, this would be in cubic inches.) If you have plenty of cubes, your child could see if he can build another shape using the same number of cubes. This activity could be repeated with 12, 16, 18, and 20 cubes.

More Cubes. Here is another activity demonstrating cubic volume using cubes and a number of small boxes of different sizes (labeled *A, B, C,* and so on). Have your child stack the cubes evenly layer by layer in one of the boxes. When the box is full, the cubes can be removed and counted. The total number of cubes is the volume of the box. Go through the same procedure with each box, and compare the results. The conclusion your child should come up with is that the bigger the box, the larger is the cubic volume.

Measure It. Measuring the perimeter of his bedroom and calculating the area can be a lot of fun for your child, who naturally may have a sense of ownership for this space. However, if the room is irregular, he may want to choose another room in the house. Have your child record his findings on centimeter graph paper. At this age it is simpler for your child to measure to the nearest foot. Therefore, if the measurement is 12 feet, 5 inches or below, the measurement will be rounded down to the nearest foot. If the measurement is 12 feet, 6 inches or above, it will be rounded up to the next foot. Once the dimensions have been recorded, your child can calculate the perimeter and the area.

What Tests May Ask

Standardized tests in third grade will ask straightforward questions that require your child to find the perimeter and area of simple figures. Students may be asked to find the one correct answer in a group of incorrect ones or to choose the incorrect response in a list of correct answers. There may be a "none of the above" statement as well.

Practice Skill: Perimeter, Area, and Volume

Directions: Read the following questions and select the correct answer.

Example:

What is the area of this shape? (Area = length × width.)

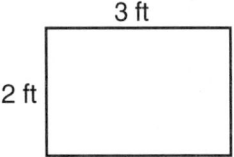

- Ⓐ 6 square feet
- Ⓑ 2 square feet
- Ⓒ 3 square feet
- Ⓓ 6 square inches

Answer:

- Ⓐ 6 square feet

8 What is the area of this shape?

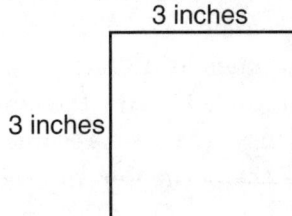

- Ⓐ 3 square inches
- Ⓑ 9 square inches
- Ⓒ 6 square inches
- Ⓓ 8 square inches

9 What is the perimeter of this shape?

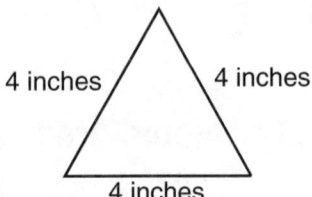

- Ⓐ 4 inches
- Ⓑ 12 inches
- Ⓒ 8 inches
- Ⓓ 6 inches

10 Choose the measurement you would need to know to lay tile on a bathroom floor.
- Ⓐ volume
- Ⓑ perimeter
- Ⓒ length
- Ⓓ area

11 How many stars would fit around the perimeter of the shape below?

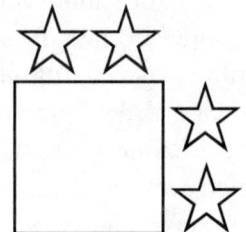

- Ⓐ 8 stars
- Ⓑ 4 stars
- Ⓒ 10 stars
- Ⓓ 6 stars

(See page 91 for answer key.)

CHAPTER 10

Measurements

By third grade, students are taught customary measurements, which until recent years were referred to as *standard measurement*. Students are also taught the metric system of measurements, although they have little exposure to this system outside the classroom unless they travel abroad. Still, it's important for students to be familiar with the terminology and develop a feel for the two standards of measurement.

Students will soon discover that the metric system is the international form of measurement in the sciences, so it's to their advantage to become at ease using both systems at an early age.

The study of measurement includes understanding linear measurement using the standard and metric systems, as well as the measurement of capacity, mass, area, perimeter, and temperature using both systems.

Your child will get better at understanding measurements as she completes word problems, where she will need to compare and convert from unit to unit. Estimation also will be emphasized at this level.

What Third Graders Should Know

Students usually enter third grade with experience in both customary and metric activities using rulers, yardsticks and meter sticks, scales, measuring spoons, and so on. They also will have had experience using inches and feet, pounds, cups, pints, and quarts. In third grade they will fill in many of the gaps and be introduced to both customary and metric systems of temperature.

Although measurement is reviewed throughout the school year as the class practices the many concepts of measurement, a standardized test probably will ask only a few questions on the subject.

Some textbooks teach one type of measurement system first and then cover the other, whereas other books teach both systems at once.

Third-grade students aren't expected to convert customary measurements to metric measurements or vice versa, but they are encouraged to feel comfortable using both. However, they should be able to identify the corresponding measurement in the other system, for example, to equate pounds with kilograms, inches with centimeters, and so on. By the end of third grade, students should be familiar with measuring tools and what each measures:

- Length: centimeter and inch rulers, yardsticks, meter sticks, tape measures
- Capacity: containers of various sizes
- Weight: scales
- Temperature: thermometers

Your child should understand and be able to give examples of what units of measurement to use for various objects—what objects would be measured in inches rather than in yards? What distances would you measure in miles rather than feet?

Most third graders will be comfortable with renaming customary units of length:

12 inches = 1 foot
3 feet = 1 yard
1,760 yards = 1 mile

The basic customary capacity units also will be discussed:

8 fluid ounces = 1 cup
2 cups = 1 pint
2 pints = 1 quart
4 quarts = 1 gallon

Renaming for weight also will be introduced:

16 ounces = 1 pound

In third grade, students will be expected to solve problems involving basic metric terms. While some of this work will take place in math classes, practice using metric measurements also will be a part of a school's science curriculum. Most of these activities focus on hands-on types of science experiments and are used in recording observations.

Since measurement estimations are so frequently used in daily living, it's important that students at this level have many opportunities to practice this skill. "About how long …," "About how many …," and "About how much …" should be emphasized as much as exact measurements. It's likely that the teacher will make sure the students know how to measure accurately. At this age, students can still be inconsistent in these skills. The teacher will tell your child to always place the edge of the ruler directly under the object being measured and that she should measure to the end of the object and record her findings. Very often students will be given rulers with inches on one side and centimeters on the other. Usually, third graders are asked to measure an object to the nearest inch or half inch, rounding up or down as necessary.

Students usually don't have many practical experiences to draw on when it comes to capacity in customary units. It's often challenging for them to remember the various measurements. Usually a chart will be displayed in the class showing the ratio between cups, pints, quarts, and gallons.

There are only two metric capacity units third-grade students need to remember—the liter and the milliliter. The milliliter is used to measure very small amounts of liquids.

By the time students get to third grade, they are usually familiar with the heavier units of weight—pounds and kilograms. They now learn that ounces and grams are used to weigh lighter objects. Students will learn that

1 pound = 16 ounces
1 kilogram = 1,000 grams

In the classroom, students probably will be given the opportunity to weigh different objects using both customary and metric units. Students will come to realize that the size of an object can be deceptive; sometimes small objects are dense and therefore heavy, whereas larger objects sometimes can be lighter and insubstantial.

By third grade, students should know that thermometers are the tools needed to measure temperatures—of living things, objects, and the weather. Although in the United States temperature is measured using the Fahrenheit scale, students will learn that in other countries and in science, the Celsius scale is used. Teachers often use very large models of thermometers that can be manipulated to adjust the "red mercury." Many students will know that the temperature on a thermometer is determined by seeing the level of the "red mercury" in the tube.

What You and Your Child Can Do

Helping your child get better at measuring is easy to do at home. Make sure your child knows how to use rulers, yardsticks, tape measures, measuring cups, scales, and thermometers. It's important that your child notices units of measurement in everyday life, especially when metric units are used (such as with soda bottles). Check the weight information on food packages such as cereal boxes. Discuss distances when you are driving; have your child estimate how far you have driven, a mile or 5 miles. Developing an understanding of the customary and metric systems of measurement and becoming proficient using the appropriate measuring tools are very important skills for children. They will be using them daily in one form or another for the rest of their lives.

Guess Again. Informally discuss what would be measured in miles, yards, feet, and inches—and then play the estimate game, asking your child to guess how high is that house or how far might it be from here to the corner. One of the most important abilities you can cultivate in your child is the skill of estimating various lengths, weights, capacities, and temperatures. Children only acquire this ability over time and through lots of experience.

Pooling It. The best place to practice capacity measures is outside, where your child can have fun and not worry about spilling water. A small toddler's wading pool is ideal (or use a large sink or tub indoors). The water will be easier to see and measure if you put in a few drops of food coloring. Collect the various measuring vessels and an assortment of containers, and let your child experiment. Briefly review customary and metric units, and then step back!

Projects. Let your third grader help with projects such as baking cakes or deciding how to plant daffodils. Encourage and provide projects that require exact measurements such as building a wooden bird house. It's the experience with hands-on measuring that is of more importance to your child's learning measurements at this level.

Scavenger Hunt. Your child will enjoy scavenger hunts in which she must identify objects of a certain length or height. In the process, your child also will get some hands-on practice! Try this with several siblings or when your child has a friend stay overnight.

Measure It. If your child seems to need the actual measurement practice, give her a fun list of objects to measure:

- Length of your longest strand of hair
- Length of your room
- Width of your window
- Height of your dog
- Length of your nose

Always ask for an estimate and then an actual measurement.

Weigh In. Does your child still enjoy playing with stuffed animals? Have her arrange a group of them from lightest to heaviest, and then check the estimates by weighing them with a balance scale. Mix up stuffed animals and toy cars or trucks—assemble a mixture of objects, and let your child weigh them. If there's an overnight friend, turn it into a competition—estimate the weight and see who comes closer!

Conversions. Simple renaming can be a challenge at this age. Provide a calculator for this type of regrouping, and start simple: If your dog is 2 feet long, how many inches would that be?

Take a Temperature. For this activity, get a good digital thermometer, and let your child test a glass of water, a cup of tea, the dishpan water, or her bath water. For more fun, turn it into a competition: Let your child guess the temperature of each item, and then compare that with the actual measurements.

Weather Station. To practice temperature measurement, have your child record the outside temperature three times a day for a week—for example, at 8 a.m., noon, and 4 p.m.—using

Fahrenheit and Celsius thermometers (if you have both). Your child may need help in taking the readings; have her record the readings on a chart, with dates and times. At the end of the week, she can plot a Fahrenheit and a Celsius graph and then compare them.

TV Weather. Watch the weather forecasts on TV together and discuss the terminology—or encourage your child to look at the weather forecast in the newspaper. Ask her to find the hottest or coldest place in the United States. Keep an atlas handy so that you can find various cities around the country and the world.

Long Jump. Your child may have a lot of fun practicing the long jump with friends and measuring their jumps. You probably should be there to oversee the process and show them how to measure and record the distances.

Olympic Records. To get another idea of distances, have your child look up Olympic records for the long jump and pole vault. She can then measure out the distance and get a sense of how far the champions really jumped.

What Tests May Ask

Standardized tests may present rulers, thermometers, and other devices and ask questions about measurements to determine how well children know their facts. They may give children an example and ask how to measure it or ask children to estimate the size of an object. Questions will include both those which exclude and those which ask your child to choose the correct answer from among several wrong ones.

Practice Skill: Measurement

Directions: Solve each problem below.

Example:

A foot is how many inches?

- Ⓐ 6
- Ⓑ 8
- Ⓒ 12
- Ⓓ 24

Answer:

- Ⓒ 12

---

1. How many inches is a 2-foot-long table?
   - Ⓐ 12 inches
   - Ⓑ 18 inches
   - Ⓒ 24 inches
   - Ⓓ none of the above

---

2. How many feet equal 3 yards?
   - Ⓐ 9 feet
   - Ⓑ 18 feet
   - Ⓒ 6 feet
   - Ⓓ none of the above

---

3. How many yards are equal to 12 feet?
   - Ⓐ 3 yards
   - Ⓑ 5 yards
   - Ⓒ 4 yards
   - Ⓓ none of the above

---

4. How many yards are equal to 36 inches?
   - Ⓐ 1 yard
   - Ⓑ 4 yards
   - Ⓒ 3 yards
   - Ⓓ none of the above

MEASUREMENTS

5 Which is longer, 1 centimeter or 1 meter?

- (A) 1 centimeter
- (B) 1 meter
- (C) They are equal.

6 Which is heavier, 1 pound or 16 ounces?

- (A) 1 pound
- (B) 16 ounces
- (C) They are equal.

7 How would you measure an ink pen?

- (A) in inches
- (B) in yards
- (C) in feet
- (D) in miles

8 Which is more, 1 cup or 1 pint?

- (A) 1 cup
- (B) 1 pint
- (C) They are equal.

Directions: Solve each problem.

Example:

Mrs. Smith bought 12 quarts of milk this week. How many pints of milk is this?

- (A) 23
- (B) 24
- (C) 12
- (D) 48

Answer:

- (B) 24

9 John helped his father paint the house. They used 24 quarts of paint. The paint came in gallon cans. How many gallons of paint did they use?

- (A) 3
- (B) 6
- (C) 4
- (D) 12

10 Seth and his sister Rachel made grape juice. How many pint glasses could be filled from 8 quarts of juice?

- (A) 8
- (B) 16
- (C) 32
- (D) 4

11 How many liters would the bottle in the picture below hold?

- (A) 1 liter
- (B) 10 liters
- (C) 100 liters
- (D) none of the above

55

12 About how many liters would the sink pictured below hold?

Ⓐ 2 liters
Ⓑ 20 liters
Ⓒ 200 liters
Ⓓ none of the above

13 How long is the string in this picture?

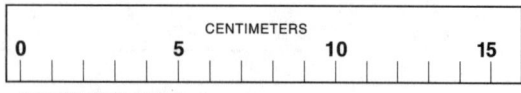

Ⓐ 5 inches
Ⓑ 5 centimeters
Ⓒ 10 inches
Ⓓ 6 centimeters

14 What might happen if the temperature outside is the same as shown on this thermometer?

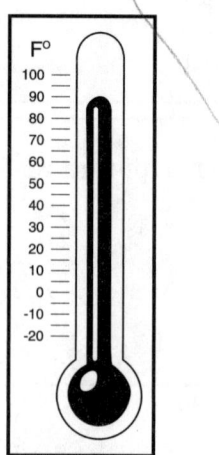

Ⓐ swimming in a pool
Ⓑ building a snowman
Ⓒ sledding
Ⓓ boiling an egg

15 Linda decided to invent a new party punch. She mixed 2 quarts of orange juice with 1 quart of grapefruit juice. Then she added 3 quarts of pineapple juice and 2 quarts of lemonade. How many gallons of punch did she make altogether?

Ⓐ 2 gallons
Ⓑ 3 gallons
Ⓒ 4 gallons
Ⓓ 1 gallon

(See page 91 for answer key.)

CHAPTER 11

Problem Solving

Problem solving is a very important part of the third-grade curriculum. Learning how to compute numbers is of little use to a child unless he also develops the skill to manipulate the numbers in such a way that they can be of practical use in his daily life. It's particularly important that students become comfortable approaching problem solving in a confident manner. Too often, as students progress, they develop a negative attitude toward this part of the curriculum. They find it challenging, and often think they aren't any good at it.

Luckily, third graders are by nature inclined to be upbeat and eager to try anything if they are encouraged and the material is interesting. They are beginning to think things through in a logical way and to develop analytical skills—so this is an ideal age to begin introducing students to a variety of problem-solving strategies.

It's important to see that your child keeps a positive attitude toward the more challenging aspects of math. Never say, "Oh, I was hopeless at math in school!" in front of your child. Children pick up on these messages all too quickly. You also should remember that children's analytical thinking skills develop at different rates. If your child finds it hard to conceptualize certain problems even with your help, let it go. Your child is not developmentally ready for it. In a matter of months, perhaps he will be.

What Third Graders Should Know

Students will have been exposed to problem-solving activities as they move up through school; by the end of second grade, they will have worked with simple one-step concrete problems. Some advanced students may have progressed to two-step problems.

During third grade, students will be presented continually with problem-solving activities. At times, these will be in the form of verbal problems presented by the teacher for the whole class to solve. These days, many math programs suggest starting the math class with a problem-solving activity. This gives the students constant practice and feedback from the teacher. Many schools encourage students to work together in small groups to find a solution to a problem.

Students also will be given more formal written word problems to which they must respond in writing, demonstrating how they arrive at a solution. The various topics they cover during the year will be tied closely to problem solving. Students are encouraged to explore solving problems using more than one method; they learn that there can be a number of different ways to find the solution to a problem. Visual learners will be more likely to make drawings, tables, and graphs, whereas analytical students are more likely to figure out the solution mathematically.

Most students are taught a simple attack plan when solving word problems:

1. Read.
2. Plan.
3. Solve.
4. Look back.

Read. Students are taught to read the problem carefully (aloud is best). The child asks himself: "What is the question I'm being asked to solve?" He must then find the key words to the problem, which will help him choose an operation.

Plan. Your child must ask himself what he must do to solve the problem. He locates the facts he needs to find a solution and chooses a strategy that he thinks may work. Sometimes a child will be presented with a two-step problem and needs to answer a hidden question before he can answer the question asked in the problem.

Solve. Your child writes down the mathematical operation he will use as a number sentence. At times he will want to first estimate the answer: Does it look reasonable? Then he must solve the problem.

Look Back. Your child should then check his work. Has he answered the question? Does the answer make sense?

Students learn to focus on key words in a question, and this helps them decide the correct mathematical operation to use. For example, addition and multiplication are operations where numbers are joined together and where such phrases as *total number, in all,* and *all together* are used in the question.

In the case of multiplication, students should be aware that equal groups are being combined and that addition is used when different numbers are being combined.

Subtraction is an operation where the difference between two numbers is found. It is indicated by *How many are left? How many remain? What is the difference?* or *Compare two numbers.*

Division is an operation that tells how many groups there are or how many are in each group. It is associated with words such as *in each, each get split evenly,* or *shared evenly.*

Usually students are comfortable using all four operations to solve problems by the last months of third grade. As the year progresses, students will be given two-step or multistep problems. Two different operations are used to solve two-step problems. If there is extra information in the problem, students should simply cross out the information that isn't important in the solution.

Sometimes students are given a problem that doesn't have enough information to allow a solution. They should be able to explain what information is missing. Sometimes students are given problems that don't have numbers. They need to use logical thinking, read or listen carefully to the problem, and draw a picture. As the student reads or hears the clues, he should keep adding to the picture.

Many third-grade teachers also discuss other problem-solving strategies, such as *guess, test, and revise.* In this method, students first make a calculated guess to find the answer. Then they test the answer to see if it's correct. If it's incorrect, the wrong guess might help them find the correct answer.

Sometimes students are shown pictures or text with information in posters, billboards, or charts. The students need to read them carefully and refer back to them to select appropriate information to solve word problems successfully. It can be quite challenging for some children to filter through the wealth of information they are presented with to find the appropriate facts.

Numbers of examples of problem-solving activities have been used and explained in earlier chapters. The emphasis in schools and on standardized tests today is to concentrate on how to solve the problem.

What You and Your Child Can Do

Parents can provide an ideal environment for children to develop their problem-solving skills. You can involve your child in everyday situations in which he sees you using skills to solve problems.

Shopping. Take your child shopping and involve him in your purchases. Keep a calculator handy in your pocket to compare prices of food, clothing, toys, and so on. Discuss the merits and disadvantages of buying certain things. Help your child locate a good bargain and calculate the bill—either by estimating or by using a calculator. Then he can compare his total with the official one. This is a good time to give a simple explanation of state sales tax.

Fast Food. When visiting a fast-food restaurant, give your child a $5 bill and let him calculate what he can order and still get some change.

Math Around the House. Involve your child in projects and decision making around your house and garden. Do we have room in your bedroom for this table? Can we plant four rows of beans in this space? How long will it take to put out the trash? We have 36 jelly beans left in the jar. Can we share them equally, or will there be some left over?

Travel On. Going on vacation provides a wealth of opportunity for informal problem solving, which also can be lots of fun. Involve your child in the planning. Let him see travel brochures and compare various vacations. Share schedules for flights, trains, or buses. If you're touring, have your child keep a family log and record how far you travel each day. The possibilities are endless, but be careful not to make your questions too complicated or to belabor the topic. Nothing can turn a child off more! Keep the tone light, and be prepared to move on to something else.

Games. Card games and board games such as Monopoly, chess, or checkers all help to develop your child's strategic and logical thinking skills. Many of these games can be played repeatedly without getting boring. Gradually, you'll see your child acquire strategies that will enhance his play. Discussing in a casual way the various strategies used by players in a game can help—as long as it doesn't get too critical. Praise clever moves. If appropriate, ask your child to explain how he thought through various moves.

If Your Child Has Trouble. If you think your child is having trouble with word problems at school, it probably will be obvious when he tackles a homework assignment. You child's teacher probably will have helpful suggestions. There are also specific ways you can help build your child's confidence in his ability to solve problems.

Because your child's full attention should be focused on how to solve the problem rather than on worrying about the calculations, it's a good idea to let him use a calculator. Make sure your child is breaking down a problem into manageable parts. Using the "read, plan, solve, and look back method" will help.

Guide your child through a problem, one step at a time, by asking appropriate questions as you proceed. You may need to work through numbers of problems before he becomes really confident. But make sure your child is doing the thinking and that you are just a helpful guide!

Find out if your child understands the *key clue words* in a problem—this will help him decide what operation to use. If he isn't familiar with these clue words, point them out. You can make a chart for your child to refer to if you wish.

Sometimes if your child is struggling with a word problem, it can help to reduce the number. In other words: "Mrs. Green received 246 red roses. She needs to put these in bunches. Each bunch will have 6 roses in it. How many bunches will she have?"

Have your child substitute "12 roses" for "246" and "3" for the "6"—it will then be much easier for your child to see what to do to solve the problem.

What Tests May Ask

Your child will not see one section of a standardized test devoted specifically to word problem solving. Instead, word problems will be scattered throughout the math portions of standardized tests, including money, measurement, addition, subtraction, multiplication, and division. The more experience in word problems your child has, the more confident he will be when facing this type of problem in standardized testing situations.

Practice Skill: Problem Solving

Directions: Read the following questions and select the correct answer.

Example:

Jenny is going camping for the weekend. She has decided to take a striped T-shirt, a yellow shirt, a red sweatshirt, navy shorts, and a pair of jeans. How many different outfits can she make from these clothes?

- Ⓐ 4
- Ⓑ 3
- Ⓒ 6
- Ⓓ 7

Answer:

- Ⓒ 6

1. Billy and his family are going to spend a week's vacation with his grandparents in Washington, D.C. They live 358 miles away. How many miles will the family travel there and back?

   - Ⓐ 716
   - Ⓑ 616
   - Ⓒ 358
   - Ⓓ 708

2. Mr. Herr decided to wash all the windows of his house. On both the front and the back of the house, there are 5 windows. On one side of the house, there are 7 windows. On the other side of the house, there are 6 windows. How many windows does Mr. Herr have to wash all together?

   - Ⓐ 20
   - Ⓑ 23
   - Ⓒ 18
   - Ⓓ 24

3. Emily and her brother ate 24 candies. Her brother gobbled down twice as many as Emily. How many candies did Emily eat?

   - Ⓐ 10
   - Ⓑ 12
   - Ⓒ 8
   - Ⓓ 14

4. Ashley had 76 silver beads. She decided to use the beads to make necklaces for her friends. She threaded 9 beads onto each necklace. How many necklaces did she make? Did she have any beads left over, and if so, how many?

   - Ⓐ 9 r 6
   - Ⓑ 8 r 4
   - Ⓒ 8
   - Ⓓ 7 r 4

PROBLEM SOLVING

5 The third-grade classes were the first in the lunchroom. Six students sat at each table. The third-grade classes filled 7 tables. Another 33 students entered the lunchroom. How many students were there now in the lunchroom?

Ⓐ 66
Ⓑ 65
Ⓒ 74
Ⓓ 75

(See page 91 for answer key.)

APPENDIX A

Web Sites and Resources for More Information

Homework

Homework Central
http://www.HomeworkCentral.com
Terrific site for students, parents, and teachers, filled with information, projects, and more.

Win the Homework Wars
(Sylvan Learning Centers)
http://www.educate.com/online/qa_peters.html

Reading and Grammar Help

Born to Read: How to Raise a Reader
http://www.ala.org/alsc/raise_a_reader.html

Guide to Grammar and Writing
http://webster.commnet.edu/hp/pages/darling/grammar.htm
Help with "plague words and phrases," grammar FAQs, sentence parts, punctuation, rules for common usage.

Internet Public Library: Reading Zone
http://www.ipl.org/cgi-bin/youth/youth.out

Keeping Kids Reading and Writing
http://www.tiac.net/users/maryl/

U.S. Dept. of Education: Helping Your Child Learn to Read
http://www.ed.gov/pubs/parents/Reading/index.html

Math Help

Center for Advancement of Learning
http://www.muskingum.edu/%7Ecal/database/Math2.html
Substitution and memory strategies for math.

Center for Advancement of Learning
http://www.muskingum.edu/%7Ecal/database/Math1.html
General tips and suggestions.

Math.com
http://www.math.com
The world of math online.

Math.com
http://www.math.com/student/testprep.html
Get ready for standardized tests.

Math.com: Homework Help in Math
http://www.math.com/students/homework.html

Math.com: Math for Homeschoolers
http://www.math.com/parents/homeschool.html

The Math Forum: Problems and Puzzles
http://forum.swarthmore.edu/library/resource_types/problems_puzzles
Lots of fun math puzzles and problems for grades K through 12.

The Math Forum: Math Tips and Tricks
http://forum.swarthmore.edu/k12/mathtips/mathtips.html

Tips on Testing

Books on Test Preparation
http://www.testbooksonline.com/preHS.asp
This site provides printed resources for parents who wish to help their children prepare for standardized school tests.

Core Knowledge Web Site
http://www.coreknowledge.org/
Site dedicated to providing resources for parents; based on the books of E. D. Hirsch, Jr., who wrote the *What Your X Grader Needs to Know* series.

Family Education Network
http://www.familyeducation.com/article/0,1120,1-6219,00.html
This report presents some of the arguments against current standardized testing practices in the public schools. The site also provides links to family activities that help kids learn.

Math.com
http://www.math.com/students/testprep.html
Get ready for standardized tests.

Standardized Tests
http://arc.missouri.edu/k12/
K through 12 assessment tools and know-how.

Parents: Testing in Schools

KidSource: Talking to Your Child's Teacher about Standardized Tests
http://www.kidsource.com/kidsource/content2/talking.assessment.k12.4.html
This site provides basic information to help parents understand their children's test results and provides pointers for how to discuss the results with their children's teachers.

eSCORE.com: State Test and Education Standards
http://www.eSCORE.com
Find out if your child meets the necessary requirements for your local schools. A Web site with experts from Brazelton Institute and Harvard's Project Zero.

Overview of States' Assessment Programs
http://ericae.net/faqs/

**Parent Soup
Education Central: Standardized Tests**
http://www.parentsoup.com/edcentral/testing
A parent's guide to standardized testing in the schools, written from a parent advocacy standpoint.

National Center for Fair and Open Testing, Inc. (FairTest)
342 Broadway
Cambridge, MA 02139
(617) 864-4810
http://www.fairtest.org

National Parent Information Network
http://npin.org

Publications for Parents from the U.S. Department of Education
http://www.ed.gov/pubs/parents/
An ever-changing list of information for parents available from the U.S. Department of Education.

State of the States Report
http://www.edweek.org/sreports/qc99/states/indicators/in-intro.htm
A report on testing and achievement in the 50 states.

Testing: General Information

Academic Center for Excellence
http://www.acekids.com

American Association for Higher Education Assessment
http://www.aahe.org/assessment/web.htm

American Educational Research Association (AERA)
http://aera.net
An excellent link to reports on American education, including reports on the controversy over standardized testing.

American Federation of Teachers
555 New Jersey Avenue, NW
Washington, D.C. 20011

APPENDIX A

Association of Test Publishers Member Products and Services
http://www.testpublishers.org/memserv.htm

Education Week on the Web
http://www.edweek.org

ERIC Clearinghouse on Assessment and Evaluation
1131 Shriver Lab
University of Maryland
College Park, MD 20742
http://ericae.net
A clearinghouse of information on assessment and education reform.

FairTest: The National Center for Fair and Open Testing
http://fairtest.org/facts/ntfact.htm
http://fairtest.org/
The National Center for Fair and Open Testing is an advocacy organization working to end the abuses, misuses, and flaws of standardized testing and to ensure that evaluation of students and workers is fair, open, and educationally sound. This site provides many links to fact sheets, opinion papers, and other sources of information about testing.

National Congress of Parents and Teachers
700 North Rush Street
Chicago, Illinois 60611

National Education Association
1201 16th Street, NW
Washington, DC 20036

National School Boards Association
http://www.nsba.org
A good source for information on all aspects of public education, including standardized testing.

Testing Our Children: A Report Card on State Assessment Systems
http://www.fairtest.org/states/survey.htm
Report of testing practices of the states, with graphical links to the states and a critique of fair testing practices in each state.

Trends in Statewide Student Assessment Programs: A Graphical Summary
http://www.ccsso.org/survey96.html
Results of annual survey of states' departments of public instruction regarding their testing practices.

U.S. Department of Education
http://www.ed.gov/

Web Links for Parents Who Want to Help Their Children Achieve
http://www.liveandlearn.com/learn.html
This page offers many Web links to free and for-sale information and materials for parents who want to help their children do well in school. Titles include such free offerings as the Online Colors Game and questionnaires to determine whether your child is ready for school.

What Should Parents Know about Standardized Testing in the Schools?
http://www.rusd.k12.ca.us/parents/standard.html
An online brochure about standardized testing in the schools, with advice regarding how to become an effective advocate for your child.

Test Publishers Online

ACT: Information for Life's Transitions
http://www.act.org

American Guidance Service, Inc.
http://www.agsnet.com

Ballard & Tighe Publishers
http://www.ballard-tighe.com

Consulting Psychologists Press
http://www.cpp-db.com

CTB McGraw-Hill
http://www.ctb.com

Educational Records Bureau
http://www.erbtest.org/index.html

Educational Testing Service
http://www.ets.org

General Educational Development (GED) Testing Service
http://www.acenet.edu/calec/ged/home.html

Harcourt Brace Educational Measurement
http://www.hbem.com

Piney Mountain Press—A Cyber-Center for Career and Applied Learning
http://www.pineymountain.com

ProEd Publishing
http://www.proedinc.com

Riverside Publishing Company
http://www.hmco.com/hmco/riverside

Stoelting Co.
http://www.stoeltingco.com

Sylvan Learning Systems, Inc.
http://www.educate.com

Touchstone Applied Science Associates, Inc. (TASA)
http://www.tasa.com

Tests Online

(*Note:* We don't endorse tests; some may not have technical documentation. Evaluate the quality of any testing program before making decisions based on its use.)

Edutest, Inc.
http://www.edutest.com
Edutest is an Internet-accessible testing service that offers criterion-referenced tests for elementary school students, based upon the standards for K through 12 learning and achievement in the states of Virginia, California, and Florida.

Virtual Knowledge
http://www.smarterkids.com
This commercial service, which enjoys a formal partnership with Sylvan Learning Centers, offers a line of skills assessments for preschool through grade 9 for use in the classroom or the home. For free online sample tests, see the Virtual Test Center.

APPENDIX B

Read More about It

Abbamont, Gary W. *Test Smart: Ready-to-Use Test-Taking Strategies and Activities for Grades 5–12.* Upper Saddle River, NJ: Prentice Hall Direct, 1997.

Cookson, Peter W., and Joshua Halberstam. *A Parent's Guide to Standardized Tests in School: How to Improve Your Child's Chances for Success.* New York: Learning Express, 1998.

Frank, Steven, and Stephen Frank. *Test-Taking Secrets: Study Better, Test Smarter, and Get Great Grades (The Backpack Study Series).* Holbrook, MA: Adams Media Corporation, 1998.

Gilbert, Sara Dulaney. *How to Do Your Best on Tests: A Survival Guide.* New York: Beech Tree Books, 1998.

Gruber, Gary. *Dr. Gary Gruber's Essential Guide to Test-Taking for Kids, Grades 3–5.* New York: William Morrow & Co., 1986.

———. *Gary Gruber's Essential Guide to Test-Taking for Kids, Grades 6, 7, 8, 9.* New York: William Morrow & Co., 1997.

Leonhardt, Mary. *99 Ways to Get Kids to Love Reading and 100 Books They'll Love.* New York: Crown, 1997.

———. *Parents Who Love Reading, Kids Who Don't: How It Happens and What You Can Do about It.* New York: Crown, 1995.

McGrath, Barbara B. *The Baseball Counting Book.* Watertown, MA: Charlesbridge, 1999.

———. *More M&M's Brand Chocolate Candies Math.* Watertown, MA: Charlesbridge, 1998.

Mokros, Janice R. *Beyond Facts & Flashcards: Exploring Math with Your Kids.* Portsmouth, NH: Heinemann, 1996.

Romain, Trevor, and Elizabeth Verdick. *True or False?: Tests Stink!* Minneapolis: Free Spirit Publishing Co., 1999.

Schartz, Eugene M. *How to Double Your Child's Grades in School: Build Brilliance and Leadership into Your Child—from Kindergarten to College—in Just 5 Minutes a Day.* New York: Barnes & Noble, 1999.

Taylor, Kathe, and Sherry Walton. *Children at the Center: A Workshop Approach to Standardized Test Preparation, K–8.* Portsmouth, NH: Heinemann, 1998.

Tobia, Sheila. *Overcoming Math Anxiety.* New York: W. W. Norton & Company, Inc., 1995.

Tufariello, Ann Hunt. *Up Your Grades: Proven Strategies for Academic Success.* Lincolnwood, IL: VGM Career Horizons, 1996.

Vorderman, Carol. *How Math Works.* Pleasantville, NY: Reader's Digest Association, Inc., 1996.

Zahler, Kathy A. *50 Simple Things You Can Do to Raise a Child Who Loves to Read.* New York: IDG Books, 1997.

APPENDIX C

What Your Child's Test Scores Mean

Several weeks or months after your child has taken standardized tests, you will receive a report such as the TerraNova Home Report found in Figures 1 and 2. You will receive similar reports if your child has taken other tests. We briefly examine what information the reports include.

Look at the first page of the Home Report. Note that the chart provides labeled bars showing the child's performance. Each bar is labeled with the child's National Percentile for that skill area. When you know how to interpret them, national percentiles can be the most useful scores you encounter on reports such as this. Even when you are confronted with different tests that use different scale scores, you can always interpret percentiles the same way, regardless of the test. A percentile tells the percent of students who score at or below that level. A percentile of 25, for example, means that 25 percent of children taking the test scored at or below that score. (It also means that 75 percent of students scored above that score.) Note that the average is always at the 50th percentile.

On the right side of the graph on the first page of the report, the publisher has designated the ranges of scores that constitute average, above average, and below average. You can also use this slightly more precise key for interpreting percentiles:

PERCENTILE RANGE	LEVEL
2 and Below	Deficient
3–8	Borderline
9–23	Low Average
24–75	Average
76–97	High Average
98 and Up	Superior

The second page of the Home report provides a listing of the child's strengths and weaknesses, along with keys for mastery, partial mastery, and non-mastery of the skills. Scoring services determine these breakdowns based on the child's scores as compared with those from the national norm group.

Your child's teacher or guidance counselor will probably also receive a profile report similar to the TerraNova Individual Profile Report, shown in Figures 3 and 4. That report will be kept in your child's permanent record. The first aspect of this report to notice is that the scores are expressed both numerically and graphically.

First look at the score bands under National Percentile. Note that the scores are expressed as bands, with the actual score represented by a dot within each band. The reason we express the scores as bands is to provide an idea of the amount by which typical scores may vary for each student. That is, each band represents a

MATH, GRADE THREE: GET READY!

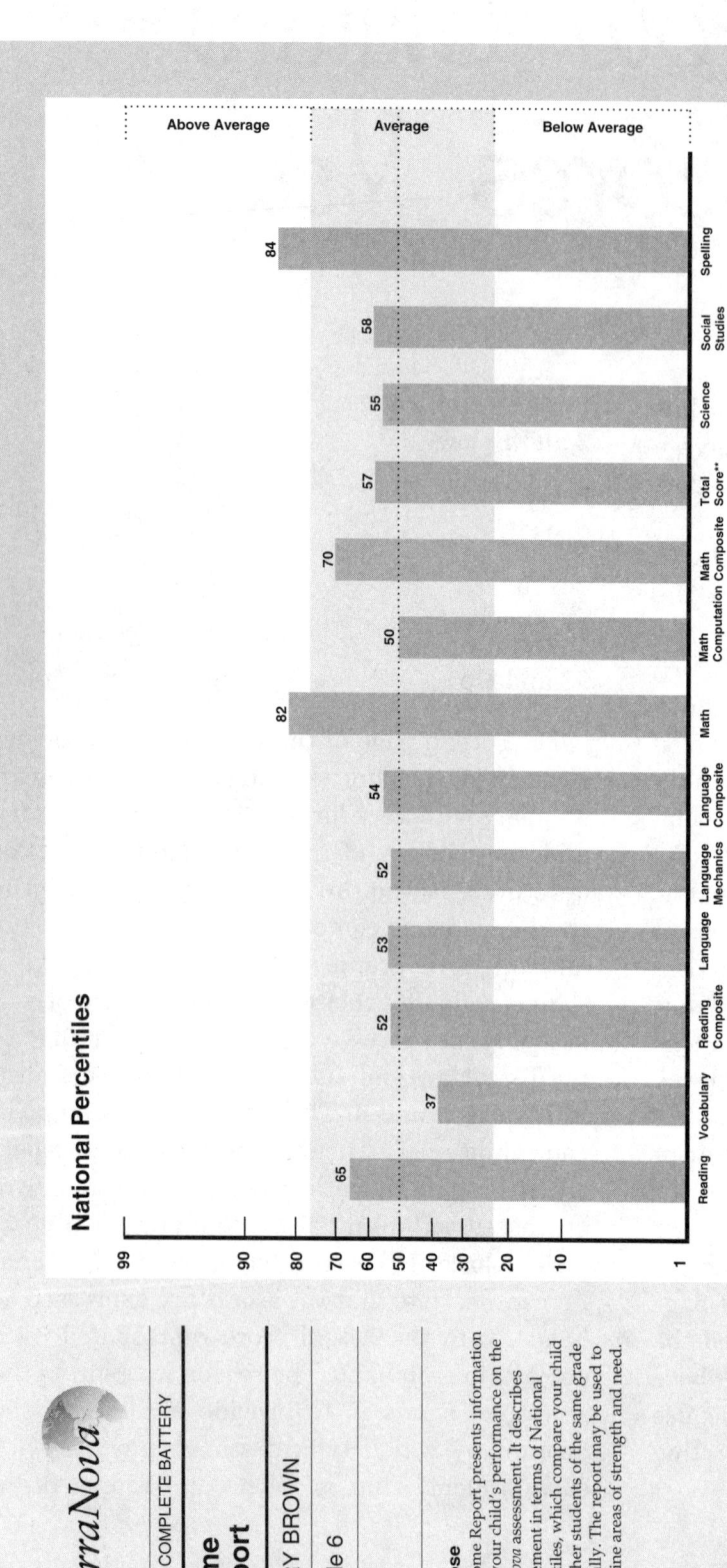

Figure 1 (SOURCE: CTB/McGraw-Hill, copyright © 1997. All rights reserved. Reproduced with permission.)

APPENDIX C

TerraNova

CTBS COMPLETE BATTERY

Home Report

MARY BROWN

Grade 6

Purpose

This page of the Home Report presents information about your child's strengths and needs. This information is provided to help you monitor your child's academic growth.

Simulated Data

Birthdate: 02/08/85
Special Codes:
A B C D E F G H I J K L M N O P Q R S T
3 5 9 7 3 2   1 1 1
Form/Level: A-16   Scoring: PATTERN (IRT)
Test Date: 11/01/99   Norms Date: 1996
QM: 08

Class: PARKER
School: WINFIELD
District: WINFIELD

City/State: WINFIELD, CA

CTB McGraw-Hill

Strengths

Reading
● Basic Understanding
● Analyze Text

Vocabulary
● Word Meaning
● Words in Context

Language
● Editing Skills
● Sentence Structure

Language Mechanics
● Sentences, Phrases, Clauses

Mathematics
● Computation and Numerical Estimation
● Operation Concepts

Mathematics Computation
● Add Whole Numbers
● Multiply Whole Numbers

Science
● Life Science
● Inquiry Skills

Social Studies
● Geographic Perspectives
● Economic Perspectives

Spelling
● Vowels
● Consonants

Key ● Mastery

Needs

Reading
◐ Evaluate and Extend Meaning
○ Identify Reading Strategies

Vocabulary
○ Multimeaning Words

Language
◐ Writing Strategies

Language Mechanics
○ Writing Conventions

Mathematics
◐ Measurement
◐ Geometry and Spatial Sense

Mathematics Computation
○ Percents

Science
○ Earth and Space Science

Social Studies
◐ Historical and Cultural Perspectives

Spelling
  No area of needs were identified for this content area

Key ◐ Partial Mastery ○ Non-Mastery

General Interpretation

The left column shows your child's best areas of performance. In each case, your child has reached mastery level. The column at the right shows the areas within each test section where your child's scores are the lowest. In these cases, your child has not reached mastery level, although he or she may have reached partial mastery.

Page 2

Copyright © 1997 CTB/McGraw-Hill. All rights reserved.

Figure 2 (SOURCE: CTB/McGraw-Hill, copyright © 1997. All rights reserved. Reproduced with permission.)

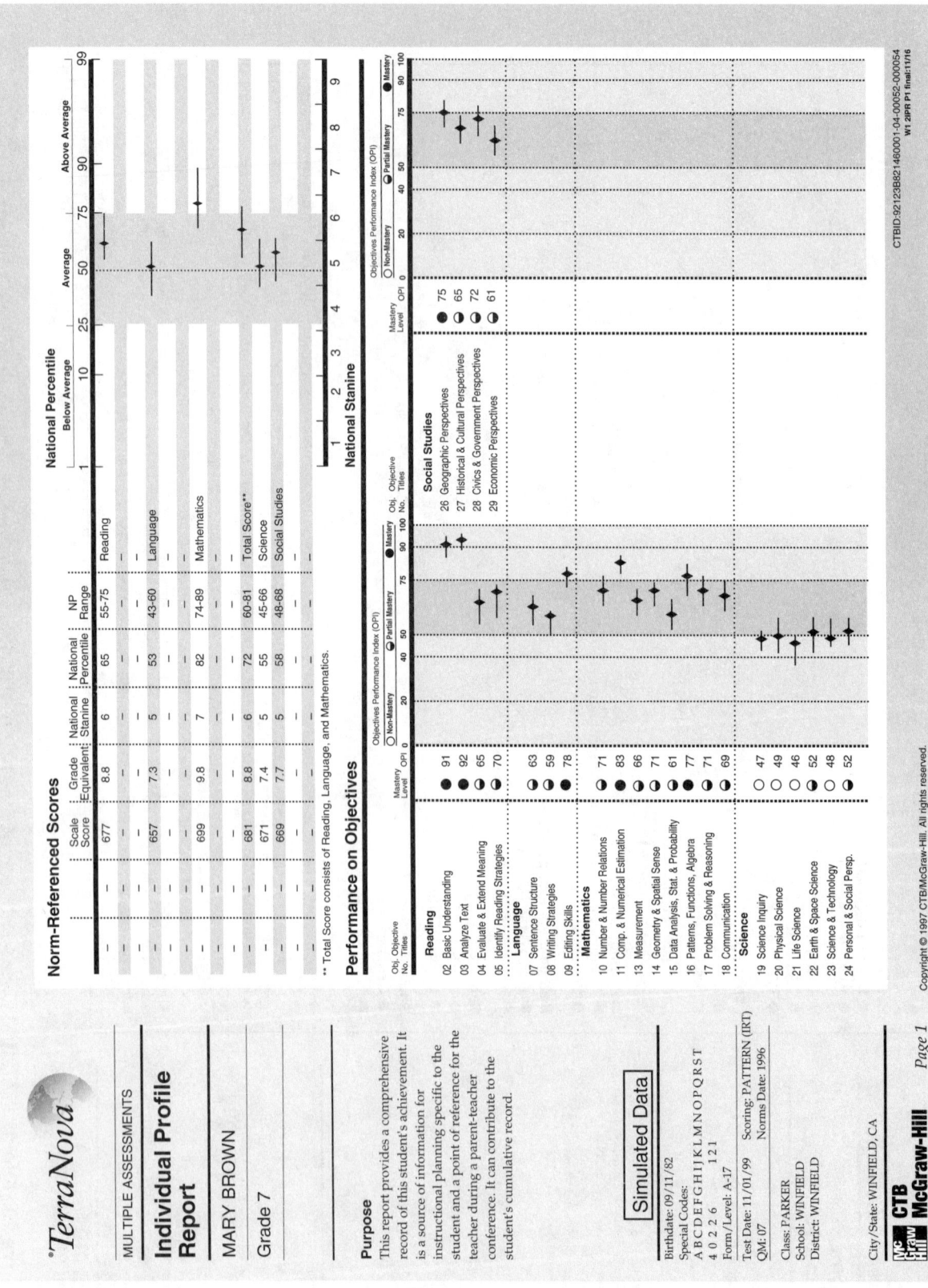

Figure 3 (Source: CTB/McGraw-Hill, copyright © 1997. All rights reserved. Reproduced with permission.)

APPENDIX C

TerraNova

MULTIPLE ASSESSMENTS

Individual Profile Report

MARY BROWN

Grade 7

Purpose

The Observations section of the Individual Profile Report gives teachers and parents information to interpret this report. This page is a narrative description of the data on the other side.

Simulated Data

Birthdate: 09/11/82
Special Codes:
A B C D E F G H I J K L M N O P Q R S T
4 0 2 2 6   1 2 1
Form/Level: A-17
Test Date: 11/01/99   Scoring: PATTERN (IRT)
QM: 08   Norms Date: 1996

Class: PARKER
School: WINFIELD
District: WINFIELD

City/State: WINFIELD, CA

CTB McGraw-Hill   Page 2   Copyright © 1997 CTB/McGraw-Hill. All rights reserved.

Observations

Norm-Referenced Scores

The top section of the report presents information about this student's achievement in several different ways. The National Percentile (NP) data and graph indicate how this student performed compared to students of the same grade nationally. The National Percentile range indicates that if this student had taken the test numerous times the scores would have fallen within the range shown. The shaded area on the graph represents the average range of scores, usually defined as the middle 50 percent of students nationally. Scores in the area to the right of the shading are above the average range. Scores in the area to the left of the shading are below the average range.

In Reading, for example, this student achieved a National Percentile rank of 65. This student scored higher than 65 percent of the students nationally. This score is in the average range. This student has a total of five scores in the average range. One score is in the above average range. No scores are in the below average range.

Performance on Objectives

The next section of the report presents performance on the objectives. Each objective is measured by a minimum of 4 items. The Objectives Performance Index (OPI) provides an estimate of the number of items that a student could be expected to answer correctly if there had been 100 items for that objective. The OPI is used to indicate mastery of each objective. An OPI of 75 and above characterizes Mastery. An OPI between 50 and 74 indicates Partial Mastery, and an OPI below 50 indicates Non-Mastery. The two-digit number preceding the objective title identifies the objective, which is fully described in the Teacher's Guide to *TerraNova*. The bands on either side of the diamonds indicate the range within which the student's test scores would fall if the student were tested numerous times.

In Reading, for example, this student could be expected to respond correctly to 91 out of 100 items measuring Basic Understanding. If this student had taken the test numerous times the OPI for this objective would have fallen between 82 and 93.

Teacher Notes

_____
_____
_____
_____
_____
_____
_____

Figure 4 (SOURCE: CTB/McGraw-Hill, copyright © 1997. All rights reserved. Reproduced with permission.)

Figure 5 (SOURCE: CTB/McGraw-Hill, copyright © 1997. All rights reserved. Reproduced with permission.)

APPENDIX C

Performance Levels (Grades 3, 4, 5)	Reading	Language	Mathematics	Science	Social Studies
5 Advanced	Students use analogies to generalize. They identify a paraphrase of concepts or ideas in texts. They can indicate thought processes that led them to a previous answer. In written responses, they demonstrate understanding of an implied theme, assess intent of passage information, and provide justification as well as support for their answers.	Students understand logical development in paragraph structure. They identify essential information from notes. They recognize the effect of prepositional phrases on subject-verb agreement. They find and correct at least 4 out of 6 errors when editing simple narratives. They correct run-on and incomplete sentences in more complex texts. They can eliminate all errors when editing their own work.	Students locate decimals on a number line; compute with decimals and fractions; read scale drawings; find areas; identify geometric transformations; construct and label bar graphs; find simple probabilities; find averages; use patterns in data to solve problems; use multiple strategies and concepts to solve unfamiliar problems; express mathematical ideas and explain the problem-solving process.	Students understand a broad range of grade level scientific concepts, such as the structure of Earth and instinctive behavior. They know terminology, such as decomposers, fossil fuel, eclipse, and buoyancy. Knowledge of more complex environmental issues includes, for example, the positive consequences of a forest fire. Students can process and interpret more detailed tables and graphs. They can suggest improvements to experimental design, such as running more trials.	Students consistently demonstrate skills such as synthesizing information from two sources (e.g., a document and a map). They show understanding of the democratic process and global environmental issues, and know the location of continents and major countries. They analyze and summarize information from multiple sources in early American history. They thoroughly explain both sides of an issue and give complete and detailed written answers to questions.
4 Proficient	Students interpret figures of speech. They recognize paraphrase of text information and retrieve information to complete forms. In more complex texts, they identify themes, main ideas, or author purpose/point of view. They analyze and apply information in graphic and text form, make reasonable generalizations, and draw conclusions. In written responses, they can identify key elements from text.	Students select the best supporting sentences for a topic sentence. They use compound predicates to combine sentences. They identify simple subjects and predicates, recognize correct usage when confronted with two types of errors, and find and correct at least 3 out of 6 errors when editing simple narratives. They can edit their own work with only minor errors.	Students compare, order, and round whole numbers; know place value to thousands; identify fractions; use computation and estimation strategies; relate multiplication to addition; measure to nearest half-inch and centimeter; measure and find perimeters; estimate measures; find elapsed times; combine and subdivide shapes; identify parallel lines; interpret tables and graphs; solve two-step problems.	Students have a range of specific science knowledge, including details about animal adaptations and classification, states of matter, and the geology of Earth. They recognize scientific words such as habitat, gravity, and mass. They understand the usefulness of computers. They understand reasons for conserving natural resources. Understanding of experimentation includes analyzing purpose, interpreting data, and selecting tools to gather data.	Students demonstrate skills in organizing information. They use time lines, product and global maps, and cardinal directions. They understand simple cause and effect relationships and historical documents. They sequence major events, associate holidays with events, and classify natural resources. They compare life in different times and understand some economic concepts related to products, jobs, and the environment. They give some detail in written responses.
3 Nearing Proficiency	Students use context clues and structural analysis to determine word meaning. They recognize homonyms and antonyms in grade-level text. They identify important details, sequence, cause and effect, and lessons embedded in the text. They interpret characters' feelings and apply information to new situations. In written responses, they can express an opinion and support it.	Students identify irrelevant sentences in paragraphs and select the best place to insert new information. They recognize faulty sentence construction. They can combine simple sentences with conjunctions and use simple subordination of phrases/clauses. They identify reference sources. They recognize correct conventions for dates, closings, and place names in informal correspondence.	Students identify even and odd numbers; subtract whole numbers with regrouping; multiply and divide by one-digit numbers; identify simple fractions; measure with ruler to nearest inch; tell time to nearest fifteen minutes; recognize and classify common shapes; recognize symmetry; subdivide shapes; complete bar graphs; extend numerical and geometric patterns; apply simple logical reasoning.	Students are familiar with the life cycles of plants and animals. They can identify an example of a cold-blooded animal. They infer what once existed from fossil evidence. They understand the term habitat. They understand the water cycle. They know science and society issues such as recycling and sources of pollution. They can sequence technological advances. They extrapolate data, devise a simple classification scheme, and determine the purpose of a simple experiment.	Students demonstrate simple information-processing skills such as using basic maps and keys. They recognize simple geographical terms, types of jobs, modes of transportation, and natural resources. They connect a human need with an appropriate community service. They identify some early famous presidents and know the capital of the United States. Their written answers are partially complete.
2 Progressing	Students identify synonyms for grade-level words, and use context clues to define common words. They make simple inferences and predictions based on text. They identify characters' feelings. They can transfer information from text to graphic form, or from graphic form to text. In written responses, they provide limited support for their answers.	Students identify the use of correct verb tenses and supply verbs to complete sentences. They complete paragraphs by selecting an appropriate topic sentence. They select correct adjective forms.	Students know ordinal numbers; solve coin combination problems; count by tens; add whole numbers with regrouping; have basic estimation skills; understand addition property of zero; write and identify number sentences describing simple situations; read calendars; identify appropriate measurement tools; recognize congruent figures; use simple coordinate grids; read common tables and graphs.	Students recognize that plants decompose and become part of soil. They can classify a plant as a vegetable. They recognize that camouflage relates to survival. They recognize terms such as hibernate. They have an understanding of human impact on the environment and are familiar with causes of pollution. They find the correct bar graph to represent given data and transfer data appropriate for middle elementary grades to a bar graph.	
1 Step 1 Partially Proficient	Students select pictured representations of ideas and identify stated details contained in simple texts. In written responses, they can select and transfer information from charts.	Students supply subjects to complete sentences. They identify the correct use of pronouns. They edit for the correct use of end marks and initial capital letters, and identify the correct convention for greetings in letters.	Students read and recognize numbers to 1000; identify real-world uses of numbers; add and subtract two-digit numbers without regrouping; identify addition situations; recognize and complete simple geometric and numerical patterns.	Students recognize basic adaptations for living in the water, identify an animal that is hatched from an egg, and associate an organism with its correct environment. They identify an object as metal. They have some understanding of conditions on the moon. They supply one way a computer can be useful. They associate an instrument like a telescope with a field of study.	Students are developing fundamental social studies skills such as locating and classifying basic information. They locate information in pictures and read and complete simple bar graphs related to social studies concepts and contexts. They can connect some city buildings with their functions and recognize certain historical objects.

IMPORTANT: Each performance level, depicted on the other side, indicates the student can perform the majority of what is described for that level and even more of what is described for the levels below. The student may also be capable of performing some of the things described in the next higher level, but not enough to have reached that level.

Figure 6 (SOURCE: CTB/McGraw-Hill, copyright © 1997. All rights reserved. Reproduced with permission.)

confidence interval. In these reports, we usually report either a 90 percent or 95 percent confidence interval. Interpret a confidence interval this way: Suppose we report a 90 percent confidence interval of 25 to 37. This means we estimate that, if the child took the test multiple times, we would expect that child's score to be in the 25 to 37 range 90 percent of the time.

Now look under the section titled Norm-Referenced Scores on the first page of the Individual Profile Report (Figure 3). The farthest column on the right provides the NP Range, which is the National Percentile scores represented by the score bands in the chart.

Next notice the column labeled Grade Equivalent. Theoretically, grade level equivalents equate a student's score in a skill area with the average grade placement of children who made the same score. Many psychologists and test developers would prefer that we stopped reporting grade equivalents, because they can be grossly misleading. For example, the average reading grade level of high school seniors as reported by one of the more popular tests is the eighth grade level. Does that mean that the nation's high school seniors cannot read? No. The way the test publisher calculated grade equivalents was to determine the average test scores for students in grades 4 to 6 and then simply extend the resulting prediction formula to grades 7 to 12. The result is that parents of average high school seniors who take the test in question would mistakenly believe that their seniors are reading four grade levels behind! Stick to the percentile in interpreting your child's scores.

Now look at the columns labeled Scale Score and National Stanine. These are two of a group of scores we also call *standard scores*. In reports for other tests, you may see other standard scores reported, such as Normal Curve Equivalents (NCEs), Z-Scores, and T-Scores. The IQ that we report on intelligence tests, for example, is a standard score. Standard scores are simply a way of expressing a student's scores in terms of the statistical properties of the scores from the norm group against which we are comparing the child. Although most psychologists prefer to speak in terms of standard scores among themselves, parents are advised to stick to percentiles in interpreting your child's performance.

Now look at the section of the report labeled Performance on Objectives. In this section, the test publisher reports how your child did on the various skills that make up each skills area. Note that the scores on each objective are expressed as a percentile band, and you are again told whether your child's score constitutes mastery, non-mastery, or partial mastery. Note that these scores are made up of tallies of sometimes small numbers of test items taken from sections such as Reading or Math. Because they are calculated from a much smaller number of scores than the main scales are (for example, Sentence Comprehension is made up of fewer items than overall Reading), their scores are less reliable than those of the main scales.

Now look at the second page of the Individual Profile Report (Figure 4). Here the test publisher provides a narrative summary of how the child did on the test. These summaries are computer-generated according to rules provided by the publisher. Note that the results descriptions are more general than those on the previous three report pages. But they allow the teacher to form a general picture of which students are performing at what general skill levels.

Finally, your child's guidance counselor may receive a summary report such as the TerraNova Student Performance Level Report. (See Figures 5 and 6.) In this report, the publisher explains to school personnel what skills the test assessed and generally how proficiently the child tested under each skill.

APPENDIX D

Which States Require Which Tests

Tables 1 through 3 summarize standardized testing practices in the 50 states and the District of Columbia. This information is constantly changing; the information presented here was accurate as of the date of printing of this book. Many states have changed their testing practices in response to revised accountability legislation, while others have changed the tests they use.

Table 1 State Web Sites: Education and Testing

STATE	GENERAL WEB SITE	STATE TESTING WEB SITE
Alabama	http://www.alsde.edu/	http://www.fairtest.org/states/al.htm
Alaska	www.educ.state.ak.us/	http://www.educ.state.ak.us/
Arizona	http://www.ade.state.az.us/	http://www.ade.state.az.us/standards/
Arkansas	http://arkedu.k12.ar.us/	http://www.fairtest.org/states/ar.htm
California	http://goldmine.cde.ca.gov/	http://star.cde.ca.gov/
Colorado	http://www.cde.state.co.us/index_home.htm	http://www.cde.state.co.us/index_assess.htm
Connecticut	http://www.state.ct.us/sde/	http://www.state.ct.us/sde/cmt/index.htm
Delaware	http://www.doe.state.de.us/	http://www.doe.state.de.us/aab/index.htm
District of Columbia	http://www.k12.dc.us/dcps/home.html	http://www.k12.dc.us/dcps/data/data_frame2.html
Florida	http://www.firn.edu/doe/	http://www.firn.edu/doe/sas/sasshome.htm
Georgia	http://www.doe.k12.ga.us/	http://www.doe.k12.ga.us/sla/ret/recotest.html
Hawaii	http://kalama.doe.hawaii.edu/upena/	http://www.fairtest.org/states/hi.htm
Idaho	http://www.sde.state.id.us/Dept/	http://www.sde.state.id.us/instruct/schoolaccount/statetesting.htm
Illinois	http://www.isbe.state.il.us/	http://www.isbe.state.il.us/isat/
Indiana	http://doe.state.in.us/	http://doe.state.in.us/assessment/welcome.html
Iowa	http://www.state.ia.us/educate/index.html	(Tests Chosen Locally)
Kansas	http://www.ksbe.state.ks.us/	http://www.ksbe.state.ks.us/assessment/
Kentucky	htp://www.kde.state.ky.us/	http://www.kde.state.ky.us/oaa/
Louisiana	http://www.doe.state.la.us/DOE/asps/home.asp	http://www.doe.state.la.us/DOE/asps/home.asp?I=HISTAKES
Maine	http://janus.state.me.us/education/homepage.htm	http://janus.state.me.us/education/mea/meacompass.htm
Maryland	http://www.msde.state.md.us/	http://msp.msde.state.md.us/
Massachusetts	http://www.doe.mass.edu/	http://www.doe.mass.edu/mcas/
Michigan	http://www.mde.state.mi.us/	http://www.MeritAward.state.mi.us/merit/meap/index.htm

APPENDIX D

STATE	GENERAL WEB SITE	STATE TESTING WEB SITE
Minnesota	http://www.educ.state.mn.us/	http://fairtest.org/states/mn.htm
Mississippi	http://mdek12.state.ms.us/	http://fairtest.org/states/ms.htm
Missouri	http://services.dese.state.mo.us/	http://fairtest.org/states/mo.htm
Montana	http://www.metnet.state.mt.us/	http://fairtest.org/states/mt.htm
Nebraska	http://www.nde.state.ne.us/	http://www.edneb.org/IPS/AppAccrd/ApprAccrd.html
Nevada	http://www.nde.state.nv.us/	http://www.nsn.k12.nv.us/nvdoe/reports/TerraNova.doc
New Hampshire	http://www.state.nh.us/doe/	http://www.state.nh.us/doe/Assessment/assessme(NHEIAP).htm
New Jersey	http://www.state.nj.us/education/	http://www.state.nj.us/njded/stass/index.html
New Mexico	http://sde.state.nm.us/	http://sde.state.nm.us/press/august30a.html
New York	http://www.nysed.gov/	http://www.emsc.nysed.gov/ciai/assess.html
North Carolina	http://www.dpi.state.nc.us/	http://www.dpi.state.nc.us/accountability/reporting/index.html
North Dakota	http://www.dpi.state.nd.us/dpi/index.htm	http://www.dpi.state.nd.us/dpi/reports/assess/assess.htm
Ohio	http://www.ode.state.oh.us/	http://www.ode.state.oh.us/ca/
Oklahoma	http://sde.state.ok.us/	http://sde.state.ok.us/acrob/testpack.pdf
Oregon	http://www.ode.state.or.us//	http://www.ode.state.or.us//asmt/index.htm
Pennsylvania	http://www.pde.psu.edu/	http://www.fairtest.org/states/pa.htm
Rhode Island	http://www.ridoe.net/	http://www.ridoe.net/standards/default.htm
South Carolina	http://www.state.sc.us/sde/	http://www.state.sc.us/sde/reports/terranov.htm
South Dakota	http://www.state.sd.us/state/executive/deca/	http://www.state.sd.us/state/executive/deca/TA/McRelReport/McRelReports.htm
Tennessee	http://www.state.tn.us/education/	http://www.state.tn.us/education/tsintro.htm
Texas	http://www.tea.state.tx.us/	http://www.tea.state.tx.us/student.assessment/
Utah	http://www.usoe.k12.ut.us/	http://www.usoe.k12.ut.us/eval/usoeeval.htm
Vermont	http://www.state.vt.us/educ/	http://www.fairtest.org/states/vt.htm

STATE	GENERAL WEB SITE	STATE TESTING WEB SITE
Virginia	http://www.pen.k12.va.us/Anthology/VDOE/	http://www.pen.k12.va.us/VDOE/Assessment/home.shtml
Washington	http://www.k12.wa.us/	http://www.k12.wa.us/assessment/
West Virginia	http://wvde.state.wv.us/	http://wvde.state.wv.us/
Wisconsin	http://www.dpi.state.wi.us/	http://www.dpi.state.wi.us/dpi/dltcl/eis/achfacts.html
Wyoming	http://www.k12.wy.us/wdehome.html	http://www.asme.com/wycas/index.htm

APPENDIX D

Table 2 Norm-Referenced and Criterion-Referenced Tests Administered by State

STATE	NORM-REFERENCED TEST	CRITERION-REFERENCED TEST	EXIT EXAM
Alabama	Stanford Achievement Test		Alabama High School Graduation Exam
Alaska	California Achievement Test	Alaska Benchmark Examinations	
Arizona	Stanford Achievement Test	Arizona's Instrument to Measure Standards (AIMS)	
Arkansas	Stanford Achievement Test		
California	Stanford Achievement Test	Standardized Testing and Reporting Supplement	High School Exit Exam (HSEE)
Colorado	None	Colorado Student Assessment Program	
Connecticut		Connecticut Mastery Test	
Delaware	Stanford Achievement Test	Delaware Student Testing Program	
District of Columbia	Stanford Achievement Test		
Florida	(Locally Selected)	Florida Comprehensive Assessment Test (FCAT)	High School Competency Test (HSCT)
Georgia	Stanford Achievement Test	Georgia Kindergarten Assessment Program—Revised and Criterion-Referenced Competency Tests (CRCT)	Georgia High School Graduation Tests
Hawaii	Stanford Achievement Test	Credit by Examination	Hawaii State Test of Essential Competencies
Idaho	Iowa Tests of Basic Skills/ Tests of Achievement and Proficiency	Direct Writing/Mathematics Assessment, Idaho Reading Indicator	
Illinois		Illinois Standards Achievement Tests	Prairie State Achievement Examination
Indiana		Indiana Statewide Testing for Educational Progress	
Iowa	(None)		
Kansas		(State-Developed Tests)	
Kentucky	Comprehensive Test of Basic Skills	Kentucky Core Content Tests	
Louisiana	Iowa Tests of Basic Skills	Louisiana Educational Assessment Program	Graduate Exit Exam
Maine		Maine Educational Assessment	High School Assessment Test
Maryland		Maryland School Performance Assessment Program, Maryland Functional Testing Program	

MATH, GRADE THREE: GET READY!

STATE	NORM-REFERENCED TEST	CRITERION-REFERENCED TEST	EXIT EXAM
Massachusetts		Massachusetts Comprehensive Assessment System	
Michigan		Michigan Educational Assessment Program	High School Test
Minnesota		Basic Standards Test	Profile of Learning
Mississippi	Comprehensive Test of Basic Skills	Subject Area Testing Program	Functional Literacy Examination
Missouri		Missouri Mastery and Achievement Test	
Montana	Iowa Tests of Basic Skills		
Nebraska			
Nevada	TerraNova		Nevada High School Proficiency Examination
New Hampshire		NH Educational Improvement and Assessment Program	
New Jersey		Elementary School Proficiency Test/Early Warning Test	High School Proficiency Test
New Mexico	TerraNova		New Mexico High School Competency Exam
New York		Pupil Evaluation Program/ Preliminary Competency Tests	Regents Competency Tests
North Carolina	Iowa Tests of Basic Skills	NC End of Grade Test	
North Dakota	TerraNova	ND Reading, Writing, Speaking, Listening, Math Test	
Ohio		Ohio Proficiency Tests	Ohio Proficiency Tests
Oklahoma	Iowa Tests of Basic Skills	Oklahoma Criterion-Referenced Tests	
Oregon		Oregon Statewide Assessment	
Pennsylvania		Pennsylvania System of School Assessment	
Rhode Island	Metropolitan Achievement Test	New Standards English Language Arts Reference Exam, New Standards Mathematics Reference Exam, Rhode Island Writing Assessment, and Rhode Island Health Education Assessment	
South Carolina	TerraNova	Palmetto Achievement Challenge Tests	High School Exit Exam
South Dakota	Stanford Achievement Test		
Tennessee	Tennessee Comprehensive Assessment Program	Tennessee Comprehensive Assessment Program	

APPENDIX D

STATE	NORM-REFERENCED TEST	CRITERION-REFERENCED TEST	EXIT EXAM
Texas		Texas Assessment of Academic Skills, End-of-Course Examinations	Texas Assessment of Academic Skills
Utah	Stanford Achievement Test	Core Curriculum Testing	
Vermont		New Standards Reference Exams	
Virginia	Stanford Achievement Test	Virginia Standards of Learning	Virginia Standards of Learning
Washington	Iowa Tests of Basic Skills	Washington Assessment of Student Learning	Washington Assessment of Student Learning
West Virginia	Stanford Achievement Test		
Wisconsin	TerraNova	Wisconsin Knowledge and Concepts Examinations	
Wyoming	TerraNova	Wyoming Comprehensive Assessment System	Wyoming Comprehensive Assessment System

Table 3 Standardized Test Schedules by State

STATE	KG	1	2	3	4	5	6	7	8	9	10	11	12	COMMENT
Alabama				X	X	X	X	X	X	X	X	X	X	
Alaska				X	X		X		X			X		
Arizona			X	X	X	X	X	X	X	X	X	X	X	
Arkansas					X	X		X	X		X	X	X	
California			X	X	X	X	X	X	X	X	X	X		
Colorado				X	X	X		X	X					
Connecticut					X		X		X					
Delaware				X	X	X			X		X	X		
District of Columbia		X	X	X	X	X	X	X	X	X	X	X		
Florida				X	X	X			X		X			There is no state-mandated norm-referenced testing. However, the state collects information furnished by local districts that elect to perform norm-referenced testing. The FCAT is administered to Grades 4, 8, and 10 to assess reading and Grades 5, 8, and 10 to assess math.
Georgia	X			X	X	X	X		X		X			
Hawaii				X			X		X		X			The Credit by Examination is voluntary and is given in Grade 8 in Algebra and Foreign Languages.
Idaho				X	X	X	X	X	X	X	X	X		
Illinois				X	X	X		X	X		X	X		Exit Exam failure will not disqualify students from graduation if all other requirements are met.
Indiana				X			X		X		X			
Iowa		*	*	*	*	*	*	*	*	*	*	*	*	*Iowa does not currently have a statewide testing program. Locally chosen assessments are administered to grades determined locally.
Kansas				X	X	X		X	X		X	X		

APPENDIX D

STATE	KG	1	2	3	4	5	6	7	8	9	10	11	12	COMMENT
Kentucky					X	X	X	X	X	X	X	X	X	
Louisiana				X	X	X	X	X	X	X	X	X	X	
Maine					X				X			X		
Maryland				X		X			X	X	X	X	X	
Massachusetts				X	X	X		X	X	X	X			
Michigan					X	X		X	X					
Minnesota					X		X		X	X	X	X	X	
Mississippi				X	X	X	X	X	X					Mississippi officials would not return phone calls or emails regarding this information.
Missouri			X	X	X	X	X	X	X	X	X			
Montana					X				X			X		The State Board of Education has decided to use a single norm-referenced test statewide beginning 2000–2001 school year.
Nebraska		**	**	**	**	**	**	**	**	**	**	**	**	**Decisions regarding testing are left to the individual school districts.
Nevada					X				X					Districts choose whether and how to test with norm-referenced tests.
New Hampshire				X			X				X			
New Jersey				X	X			X	X	X	X	X		
New Mexico					X		X		X					
New York				X	X	X	X	X	X	X			X	Assessment program is going through major revisions.
North Carolina	X			X	X	X	X		X	X			X	NRT Testing selects samples of students, not all.
North Dakota					X		X		X		X			
Ohio					X		X			X			X	
Oklahoma				X		X		X	X			X		
Oregon					X		X		X		X			

MATH, GRADE THREE: GET READY!

STATE	KG	1	2	3	4	5	6	7	8	9	10	11	12	COMMENT
Pennsylvania						X	X		X	X		X		
Rhode Island				X	X	X		X	X	X	X	X		
South Carolina				X	X	X	X	X	X	X	X	***	***	***Students who fail the High School Exit Exam have opportunities to take the exam again in grades 11 and 12.
South Dakota			X		X	X			X	X		X		
Tennessee			X	X	X	X	X	X	X					
Texas				X	X	X	X	X	X		X	X	X	
Utah		X	X	X	X	X	X	X	X	X	X	X	X	
Vermont					X	X	X		X	X	X	X		Rated by the Centers for Fair and Open Testing as a nearly model system for assessment.
Virginia				X	X	X	X		X	X		X		
Washington					X			X			X			
West Virginia				X	X	X	X	X	X	X	X	X		
Wisconsin					X				X		X			
Wyoming					X				X			X		

APPENDIX E

Testing Accommodations

The more testing procedures vary from one classroom or school to the next, the less we can compare the scores from one group to another. Consider a test in which the publisher recommends that three sections of the test be given in one 45-minute session per day on three consecutive days. School A follows those directions. To save time, School B gives all three sections of the test in one session lasting slightly more than two hours. We can't say that both schools followed the same testing procedures. Remember that the test publishers provide testing procedures so schools can administer the tests in as close a manner as possible to the way the tests were administered to the groups used to obtain test norms. When we compare students' scores to norms, we want to compare apples to apples, not apples to oranges.

Most schools justifiably resist making any changes in testing procedures. Informally, a teacher can make minor changes that don't alter the testing procedures, such as separating two students who talk with each other instead of paying attention to the test; letting Lisa, who is getting over an ear infection, sit closer to the front so she can hear better; or moving Jeffrey away from the window to prevent his looking out the window and daydreaming.

There are two groups of students who require more formal testing accommodations. One group of students is identified as having a disability under Section 504 of the Rehabilitation Act of 1973 (Public Law 93-112). These students face some challenge but, with reasonable and appropriate accommodation, can take advantage of the same educational opportunities as other students. That is, they have a condition that requires some accommodation for them.

Just as schools must remove physical barriers to accommodate students with disabilities, they must make appropriate accommodations to remove other types of barriers to students' access to education. Marie is profoundly deaf, even with strong hearing aids. She does well in school with the aid of an interpreter, who signs her teacher's instructions to her and tells her teacher what Marie says in reply. An appropriate accommodation for Marie would be to provide the interpreter to sign test instructions to her, or to allow her to watch a videotape with an interpreter signing test instructions. Such a reasonable accommodation would not deviate from standard testing procedures and, in fact, would ensure that Marie received the same instructions as the other students.

If your child is considered disabled and has what is generally called a Section 504 Plan or individual accommodation plan (IAP), then the appropriate way to ask for testing accommodations is to ask for them in a meeting to discuss school accommodations under the plan. If your child is not already covered by such a plan, he or she won't qualify for one merely because you request testing accommodations.

The other group of students who may receive formal testing accommodations are those identified as handicapped under the Individuals with Disabilities Education Act (IDEA)—students with mental retardation, learning disabilities, serious emotional disturbance, orthopedic handicap, hearing or visual problems, and other handicaps defined in the law. These students have been identified under procedures governed by federal and sometimes state law, and their education is governed by a document called the Individualized Educational Program (IEP). Unless you are under a court order specifically revoking your educational rights on behalf of your child, you are a full member of the IEP team even if you and your child's other parent are divorced and the other parent has custody. Until recently, IEP teams actually had the prerogative to exclude certain handicapped students from taking standardized group testing altogether. However, today states make it more difficult to exclude students from testing.

If your child is classified as handicapped and has an IEP, the appropriate place to ask for testing accommodations is in an IEP team meeting. In fact, federal regulations require IEP teams to address testing accommodations. You have the right to call a meeting at any time. In that meeting, you will have the opportunity to present your case for the accommodations you believe are necessary. Be prepared for the other team members to resist making extreme accommodations unless you can present a very strong case. If your child is identified as handicapped and you believe that he or she should be provided special testing accommodations, contact the person at your child's school who is responsible for convening IEP meetings and request a meeting to discuss testing accommodations.

Problems arise when a request is made for accommodations that cause major departures from standard testing procedures. For example, Lynn has an identified learning disability in mathematics calculation and attends resource classes for math. Her disability is so severe that her IEP calls for her to use a calculator when performing all math problems. She fully understands math concepts, but she simply can't perform the calculations without the aid of a calculator. Now it's time for Lynn to take the school-based standardized tests, and she asks to use a calculator. In this case, since her IEP already requires her to be provided with a calculator when performing math calculations, she may be allowed a calculator during school standardized tests. However, because using a calculator constitutes a major violation of standard testing procedures, her score on all sections in which she is allowed to use a calculator will be recorded as a failure, and her results in some states will be removed from among those of other students in her school in calculating school results.

How do we determine whether a student is allowed formal accommodations in standardized school testing and what these accommodations may be? First, if your child is not already identified as either handicapped or disabled, having the child classified in either group solely to receive testing accommodations will be considered a violation of the laws governing both classifications. Second, even if your child is already classified in either group, your state's department of public instruction will provide strict guidelines for the testing accommodations schools may make. Third, even if your child is classified in either group and you are proposing testing accommodations allowed under state testing guidelines, any accommodations must still be both *reasonable* and *appropriate*. To be reasonable and appropriate, testing accommodations must relate to your child's disability and must be similar to those already in place in his or her daily educational program. If your child is always tested individually in a separate room for all tests in all subjects, then a similar practice in taking school-based standardized tests may be appropriate. But if your child has a learning disability only in mathematics calculation, requesting that all test questions be read to him or her is inappropriate because that accommodation does not relate to his identified handicap.

Glossary

Accountability The idea that a school district is held responsible for the achievement of its students. The term may also be applied to holding students responsible for a certain level of achievement in order to be promoted or to graduate.

Achievement test An assessment that measures current knowledge in one or more of the areas taught in most schools, such as reading, math, and language arts.

Aptitude test An assessment designed to predict a student's potential for learning knowledge or skills.

Content validity The extent to which a test represents the content it is designed to cover.

Criterion-referenced test A test that rates how thoroughly a student has mastered a specific skill or area of knowledge. Typically, a criterion-referenced test is subjective, and relies on someone to observe and rate student work; it doesn't allow for easy comparisons of achievement among students. Performance assessments are criterion-referenced tests. The opposite of a criterion-referenced test is a norm-referenced test.

Frequency distribution A tabulation of individual scores (or groups of scores) that shows the number of persons who obtained each score.

Generalizability The idea that the score on a test reflects what a child knows about a subject, or how well he performs the skills the test is supposed to be assessing. Generalizability requires that enough test items are administered to truly assess a student's achievement.

Grade equivalent A score on a scale developed to indicate the school grade (usually measured in months of a year) that corresponds to an average chronological age, mental age, test score, or other characteristic. A grade equivalent of 6.4 is interpreted as a score that is average for a group in the fourth month of Grade 6.

High-stakes assessment A type of standardized test that has major consequences for a student or school (such as whether a child graduates from high school or gets admitted to college).

Mean Average score of a group of scores.

Median The middle score in a set of scores ranked from smallest to largest.

National percentile Percentile score derived from the performance of a group of individuals across the nation.

Normative sample A comparison group consisting of individuals who have taken a test under standard conditions.

Norm-referenced test A standardized test that can compare scores of students in one school with a reference group (usually other students in the same grade and age, called the "norm group"). Norm-referenced tests compare the achievement of one student or the students of a school, school district, or state with the norm score.

Norms A summary of the performance of a group of individuals on which a test was standardized.

Percentile An incorrect form of the word *centile,* which is the percent of a group of scores that falls below a given score. Although the correct term is *centile,* much of the testing literature has adopted the term *percentile.*

Performance standards A level of performance on a test set by education experts.

Quartiles Points that divide the frequency distribution of scores into equal fourths.

Regression to the mean The tendency of scores in a group of scores to vary in the direction of the mean. For example: If a child has an abnormally low score on a test, she is likely to make a higher score (that is, one closer to the mean) the next time she takes the test.

Reliability The consistency with which a test measures some trait or characteristic. A measure can be reliable without being valid, but it can't be valid without being reliable.

Standard deviation A statistical measure used to describe the extent to which scores vary in a group of scores. Approximately 68 percent of scores in a group are expected to be in a range from one standard deviation below the mean to one standard deviation above the mean.

Standardized test A test that contains well-defined questions of proven validity and that produces reliable scores. Such tests are commonly paper-and-pencil exams containing multiple-choice items, true or false questions, matching exercises, or short fill-in-the-blanks items. These tests may also include performance assessment items (such as a writing sample), but assessment items cannot be completed quickly or scored reliably.

Test anxiety Anxiety that occurs in test-taking situations. Test anxiety can seriously impair individuals' ability to obtain accurate scores on a test.

Validity The extent to which a test measures the trait or characteristic it is designed to measure. Also see *reliability.*

Answer Keys for Practice Skills

Chapter 2:
Basic Number Facts
1. C
2. C
3. B
4. C
5. B
6. D

Chapter 3:
Addition
1. B
2. D
3. C
4. A
5. C
6. D
7. C

Chapter 4:
Subtraction
1. D
2. A
3. C
4. A
5. C
6. B

Chapter 5:
Multiplication
1. A
2. B
3. D
4. D
5. C
6. B
7. D
8. A

Chapter 6:
Division
1. A
2. B
3. B
4. A
5. B
6. B
7. A
8. D
9. A
10. B

Chapter 7:
Fractions and Decimals
1. C
2. B
3. C
4. A
5. B
6. A
7. C
8. D
9. A
10. D
11. C
12. D

Chapter 8:
Place Value, Number Sense, and Money
1. C
2. B
3. C
4. A
5. A
6. A
7. B
8. D

Chapter 9:
Geometry
1. C
2. C
3. C
4. B
5. D
6. D
7. B
8. B
9. B
10. D
11. A

Chapter 10:
Measurements
1. C
2. A
3. C
4. A
5. B
6. C
7. A
8. B
9. B
10. B
11. A
12. B
13. B
14. A
15. A

Chapter 11:
Problem Solving
1. A
2. B
3. C
4. B
5. D

Sample Practice Test

You may be riding a roller coaster of feelings and opinions at this point. If your child has gone through the preceding chapters easily, then you're both probably excited to move on, to jump in with both feet, take the test, and that will be that. On the other hand, your child may have struggled a bit with some of the chapters. Some of the concepts may be difficult for him and will require a little more practice. Never fear!

All children acquire skills in all areas of learning when they are developmentally ready. We can't push them, but we can reinforce the skills that they already know. In addition, we can play games and do activities to pave the way for their understanding of the skills that they will need to master later. With luck, that's what you've done with the preceding chapters.

The test that follows is designed to incorporate components of several different kinds of standardized tests. The test that your child takes in school probably won't look just like this one, but it should be sufficiently similar that he should be pretty comfortable with the format. The administration of tests varies as well. It is important that your child hear the rhythm and language used in standardized tests. If you wish, you may have your child read the directions that precede each test section to you first and explain what the item is asking him to do. Your child may try it on his own if you feel he understands it, or you may want to clarify the instructions.

Test Administration

If you like, you may complete the entire test in one day, but it is not recommended that your child attempt to finish it in one sitting. As test administrator, you'll find that you'll need to stretch, have a snack, or use the bathroom too! If you plan to do the test in one day, leave at least 15 minutes between sessions.

Before you start, prepare a quiet place, free of distractions. Have two or three sharpened pencils with erasers that don't smudge and a flat, clear work space. As your child proceeds from item to item, encourage him to ask you if he doesn't understand something. In a real testing situation, questions are accepted, but the extent to which items can be explained is limited. Don't go overboard in making sure your child understands what to do. Your child will have to learn to trust his instincts somewhat.

The test shouldn't take all day. If your youngster seems to be dawdling along, enforce time limits and help him to understand that the real test will have time limits as well. Relax, and try to have fun!

MATH, GRADE 3 NAME AND ANSWER SHEET

To the Student:

These tests will give you a chance to put the tips you have learned to work.

A few last reminders . . .

- Be sure you understand all the directions before you begin each test. You may ask the teacher questions about the directions if you do not understand them.
- Work as quickly as you can during each test.
- When you change an answer, be sure to erase your first mark completely.
- You can guess at an answer or skip difficult items and go back to them later.
- Use the tips you have learned whenever you can.
- It is OK to be a little nervous. You may even do better.

Now that you have completed the lessons in this book, you are on your way to scoring high!

Math, Grade 3 Name and Answer Sheet

Addition

1 Ⓐ Ⓑ Ⓒ Ⓓ   4 Ⓐ Ⓑ Ⓒ Ⓓ   7 Ⓐ Ⓑ Ⓒ Ⓓ   10 Ⓐ Ⓑ Ⓒ Ⓓ   13 Ⓐ Ⓑ Ⓒ Ⓓ   15 Ⓐ Ⓑ Ⓒ Ⓓ
2 Ⓐ Ⓑ Ⓒ Ⓓ   5 Ⓐ Ⓑ Ⓒ Ⓓ   8 Ⓐ Ⓑ Ⓒ Ⓓ   11 Ⓐ Ⓑ Ⓒ Ⓓ   14 Ⓐ Ⓑ Ⓒ Ⓓ   16 Ⓐ Ⓑ Ⓒ Ⓓ
3 Ⓐ Ⓑ Ⓒ Ⓓ   6 Ⓐ Ⓑ Ⓒ Ⓓ   9 Ⓐ Ⓑ Ⓒ Ⓓ   12 Ⓐ Ⓑ Ⓒ Ⓓ

Subtraction

1 Ⓐ Ⓑ Ⓒ Ⓓ   4 Ⓐ Ⓑ Ⓒ Ⓓ   7 Ⓐ Ⓑ Ⓒ Ⓓ   10 Ⓐ Ⓑ Ⓒ Ⓓ   13 Ⓐ Ⓑ Ⓒ Ⓓ   15 Ⓐ Ⓑ Ⓒ Ⓓ
2 Ⓐ Ⓑ Ⓒ Ⓓ   5 Ⓐ Ⓑ Ⓒ Ⓓ   8 Ⓐ Ⓑ Ⓒ Ⓓ   11 Ⓐ Ⓑ Ⓒ Ⓓ   14 Ⓐ Ⓑ Ⓒ Ⓓ   16 Ⓐ Ⓑ Ⓒ Ⓓ
3 Ⓐ Ⓑ Ⓒ Ⓓ   6 Ⓐ Ⓑ Ⓒ Ⓓ   9 Ⓐ Ⓑ Ⓒ Ⓓ   12 Ⓐ Ⓑ Ⓒ Ⓓ

Multiplication

1 Ⓐ Ⓑ Ⓒ Ⓓ   4 Ⓐ Ⓑ Ⓒ Ⓓ   7 Ⓐ Ⓑ Ⓒ Ⓓ   10 Ⓐ Ⓑ Ⓒ Ⓓ   13 Ⓐ Ⓑ Ⓒ Ⓓ   15 Ⓐ Ⓑ Ⓒ Ⓓ
2 Ⓐ Ⓑ Ⓒ Ⓓ   5 Ⓐ Ⓑ Ⓒ Ⓓ   8 Ⓐ Ⓑ Ⓒ Ⓓ   11 Ⓐ Ⓑ Ⓒ Ⓓ   14 Ⓐ Ⓑ Ⓒ Ⓓ   16 Ⓐ Ⓑ Ⓒ Ⓓ
3 Ⓐ Ⓑ Ⓒ Ⓓ   6 Ⓐ Ⓑ Ⓒ Ⓓ   9 Ⓐ Ⓑ Ⓒ Ⓓ   12 Ⓐ Ⓑ Ⓒ Ⓓ

Division

1 Ⓐ Ⓑ Ⓒ Ⓓ   3 Ⓐ Ⓑ Ⓒ Ⓓ   5 Ⓐ Ⓑ Ⓒ Ⓓ   7 Ⓐ Ⓑ Ⓒ Ⓓ   9 Ⓐ Ⓑ Ⓒ Ⓓ   10 Ⓐ Ⓑ Ⓒ Ⓓ
2 Ⓐ Ⓑ Ⓒ Ⓓ   4 Ⓐ Ⓑ Ⓒ Ⓓ   6 Ⓐ Ⓑ Ⓒ Ⓓ   8 Ⓐ Ⓑ Ⓒ Ⓓ

Fractions

1 Ⓐ Ⓑ Ⓒ Ⓓ   3 Ⓐ Ⓑ Ⓒ Ⓓ   5 Ⓐ Ⓑ Ⓒ Ⓓ   7 Ⓐ Ⓑ Ⓒ Ⓓ   9 Ⓐ Ⓑ Ⓒ Ⓓ   11 Ⓐ Ⓑ Ⓒ Ⓓ
2 Ⓐ Ⓑ Ⓒ Ⓓ   4 Ⓐ Ⓑ Ⓒ Ⓓ   6 Ⓐ Ⓑ Ⓒ Ⓓ   8 Ⓐ Ⓑ Ⓒ Ⓓ   10 Ⓐ Ⓑ Ⓒ Ⓓ   12 Ⓐ Ⓑ Ⓒ Ⓓ

Decimals

1 Ⓐ Ⓑ Ⓒ Ⓓ   3 Ⓐ Ⓑ Ⓒ Ⓓ   5 Ⓐ Ⓑ Ⓒ Ⓓ   7 Ⓐ Ⓑ Ⓒ Ⓓ   9 Ⓐ Ⓑ Ⓒ Ⓓ   10 Ⓐ Ⓑ Ⓒ Ⓓ
2 Ⓐ Ⓑ Ⓒ Ⓓ   4 Ⓐ Ⓑ Ⓒ Ⓓ   6 Ⓐ Ⓑ Ⓒ Ⓓ   8 Ⓐ Ⓑ Ⓒ Ⓓ

Money

1 Ⓐ Ⓑ Ⓒ Ⓓ   3 Ⓐ Ⓑ Ⓒ Ⓓ   5 Ⓐ Ⓑ Ⓒ Ⓓ   7 Ⓐ Ⓑ Ⓒ Ⓓ   9 Ⓐ Ⓑ Ⓒ Ⓓ   11 Ⓐ Ⓑ Ⓒ Ⓓ
2 Ⓐ Ⓑ Ⓒ Ⓓ   4 Ⓐ Ⓑ Ⓒ Ⓓ   6 Ⓐ Ⓑ Ⓒ Ⓓ   8 Ⓐ Ⓑ Ⓒ Ⓓ   10 Ⓐ Ⓑ Ⓒ Ⓓ   12 Ⓐ Ⓑ Ⓒ Ⓓ

Geometry

1 Ⓐ Ⓑ Ⓒ Ⓓ   4 Ⓐ Ⓑ Ⓒ Ⓓ   7 Ⓐ Ⓑ Ⓒ Ⓓ   10 Ⓐ Ⓑ Ⓒ Ⓓ   13 Ⓐ Ⓑ Ⓒ Ⓓ   15 Ⓐ Ⓑ Ⓒ Ⓓ
2 Ⓐ Ⓑ Ⓒ Ⓓ   5 Ⓐ Ⓑ Ⓒ Ⓓ   8 Ⓐ Ⓑ Ⓒ Ⓓ   11 Ⓐ Ⓑ Ⓒ Ⓓ   14 Ⓐ Ⓑ Ⓒ Ⓓ   16 Ⓐ Ⓑ Ⓒ Ⓓ
3 Ⓐ Ⓑ Ⓒ Ⓓ   6 Ⓐ Ⓑ Ⓒ Ⓓ   9 Ⓐ Ⓑ Ⓒ Ⓓ   12 Ⓐ Ⓑ Ⓒ Ⓓ

Measurement

1 Ⓐ Ⓑ Ⓒ Ⓓ   4 Ⓐ Ⓑ Ⓒ Ⓓ   7 Ⓐ Ⓑ Ⓒ Ⓓ   10 Ⓐ Ⓑ Ⓒ Ⓓ   13 Ⓐ Ⓑ Ⓒ Ⓓ   15 Ⓐ Ⓑ Ⓒ
2 Ⓐ Ⓑ Ⓒ Ⓓ   5 Ⓐ Ⓑ Ⓒ   8 Ⓐ Ⓑ Ⓒ   11 Ⓐ Ⓑ Ⓒ Ⓓ   14 Ⓐ Ⓑ Ⓒ Ⓓ
3 Ⓐ Ⓑ Ⓒ Ⓓ   6 Ⓐ Ⓑ Ⓒ   9 Ⓐ Ⓑ Ⓒ Ⓓ   12 Ⓐ Ⓑ Ⓒ Ⓓ

SAMPLE PRACTICE TEST

ADDITION

Directions: Read the following questions and select the correct answer.

Example:

    4
  +2

  A 6

  B 1

  C 7

  D 5

Answer:

  A 6

---

1.   3
    +9

  A 14

  B 12

  C 13

  D 6

---

2.   10
    +6

  A 8

  B 4

  C 2

  D 16

---

3.   6
    5
   +2

  A 13

  B 14

  C 11

  D 16

---

4. Write a family of facts for the group of numbers 5, 3, and 8.

  A 5 + 3 = 8   8 + 8 = 16
       16 − 8 = 8   5 − 8 = 3

  B 3 + 5 = 8   18 + 3 = 21
       5 + 8 = 3   3 − 3 = 0

  C 5 + 3 = 8   3 + 5 = 8
       8 − 3 = 5   8 − 5 = 3

  D 8 + 3 = 11   8 + 5 = 13
       8 − 5 = 3   8 − 3 = 5

---

5. Find the missing addend:
    10 + ___ = 14.

  A 5

  B 7

  C 4

  D 14

6 A brown dog dug a hole and buried 3 bones. Later in the day the dog came along and added another 2 bones. How many bones were there all together?

   A 5
   B 1
   C 2
   D 3

7 Barbara gathered five buckets of berries. Her friend Joan picked one bucket, and her friend Sasha picked three buckets. How many buckets of berries did the girls gather?

   A 7
   B 8
   C 9
   D none of the above

Directions: Read the following questions and select the correct answer.

Example:

   Mentally add 200 + 600.

   A 200
   B 800
   C 600
   D 2,000

Answer:

   B 800

8 Mentally add 800 and 500.

   A 1,300
   B 130
   C 13,000
   D 300

9
```
   10
   22
   67
  +31
```
   A 120
   B 130
   C 144
   D 164

10
```
   20
   13
   72
  +45
```
   A 155
   B 150
   C 255
   D 265

11 Estimate the sum of 488 + 129.

   A 1,400
   B 160
   C 600
   D 1,500

SAMPLE PRACTICE TEST

12   222
    +985

  A 1,441

  B 237

  C 1,107

  D 1,207

13 $5.34
    +8.98

  A $13.22

  B $14.32

  C $14.22

  D $12.14

14   2,514
    +7,597

  A 10,222

  B 9,017

  C 9,111

  D 10,111

15 Jared had 9 apples, and Letitia had 23 grapes. How many fruits were there all together?

  A 12

  B 6

  C 32

  D 14

16 Sally's mother made a dozen cookies for the bake sale. June's mother made another dozen cookies, and Sam's mother brought a dozen, too. How many cookies were there in all?

  A 36

  B 24

  C 12

  D none of the above

SUBTRACTION

Directions: Read the following problems and select the correct answer.

Example:

Subtract mentally: 40 − 12 = ___.

A 28

B 38

C 48

D 62

Answer:

A 28

---

1 Subtract mentally: 38 − 12 = ___.

   A 30

   B 28

   C 38

   D 26

---

2 Estimate the difference:
   622 − 281 = ___.

   A 300

   B 342

   C 400

   D 200

---

3 Estimate the difference:
   739 − 299 = ___.

   A 450

   B 400

   C 500

   D 600

---

4 Estimate the difference:
   886 − 698 = ___.

   A 200

   B 100

   C 300

   D 298

---

5 82
   −16

   A 53

   B 76

   C 66

   D 47

---

6 90
   −16

   A 74

   B 64

   C 106

   D 76

GO

SAMPLE PRACTICE TEST

7   400
   −156

   A 314
   B 300
   C 556
   D 244

8   960
   −589

   A 371
   B 389
   C 1,389
   D none of the above

9 $32.50
    −8.54

   A $23.96
   B $13.96
   C $41.04
   D $14.17

10 $52.80
    −9.23

   A $61.03
   B $43.57
   C $53.57
   D $53.47

11   9,004
   −2,947

   A 5,047
   B 6,057
   C 5,953
   D 5,146

12   1,008
    −300

   A 708
   B 608
   C 707
   D 3,407

13   7,254
    −726

   A 6,528
   B 7,980
   C 7,538
   D none of the above

14 846 − 220 = ___

   A 626
   B 1,060
   C 620
   D 826

15 John drove his car 435 miles. Suzy drove her car 2100 miles. How many more miles was Suzy's car driven than John's?

A 1665

B 2535

C 1675

D none of the above

16 There were 356 students in Jamie's school. If 213 were boys, how many were girls?

A 569

B 143

C 133

D none of the above

SAMPLE PRACTICE TEST

MULTIPLICATION

Directions: Read the following problems and select the correct answer.

Example:

    $4 \times 6 =$ ___

    A 25

    B 28

    C 24

    D 36

Answer:

    C 24

---

1 Write a number sentence for the following illustration.

    OO   OO   OO
    OO   OO   OO

    A $3 \times 4 = 9$

    B $4 + 3 = 6$

    C $4 \times 3 = 12$

    D $4 \times 6 = 28$

---

2 $7 \times 8 =$ ___

    A 64

    B 63

    C 56

    D 72

---

3   9
    $\times 4$

    A 24

    B 40

    C 32

    D 36

---

4   8
    $\times 6$

    A 24

    B 40

    C 48

    D 36

---

5   5
    $\times 6$

    A 45

    B 35

    C 30

    D 25

---

6   9
    $\times 8$

    A 56

    B 76

    C 98

    D 72

GO

7. 20
   × 0

   A 20
   B 0
   C 200
   D 2,000

8. 8 × 80 = ___

   A 7,200
   B 810
   C 169
   D 640

9. Estimate: 3 × 237 = ___.

   A 3,222
   B 600
   C 3,000
   D 300

10. 63
    × 4

    A 644
    B 254
    C 252
    D 564

11. 72
    × 3

    A 216
    B 316
    C 215
    D 221

12. 8 × 8 = ___

    A 80
    B 81
    C 90
    D 64

13. 0 × 7 = ___

    A 4
    B 0
    C 7
    D 16

14. 16
    × 3

    A 38
    B 48
    C 21
    D 11

Example:

Mr. Hammond baked 2 dozen chocolate cupcakes. How many cupcakes did he bake in all?

A 12
B 24
C 36
D 48

Answer:

B 24

SAMPLE PRACTICE TEST

15 Yoko bought 16 pens. Each pen cost $3. How much did all the pens cost?

    A $48

    B $38

    C $18

    D $28

16 Sharon loves horses. She owned 14 models of horses, and at her birthday party last week, she was given another 14. How many does she now have?

    A 46

    B 56

    C 76

    D 28

DIVISION

Directions: Complete each problem.

Example:

20 ÷ 4 = ___
- **A** 105
- **B** 5
- **C** 25
- **D** 20

Answer:

B 5

---

1 12 ÷ 3 = ___
- **A** 3
- **B** 8
- **C** 4
- **D** not given

---

2 8 ÷ 2 = ___
- **A** 6
- **B** 3
- **C** 4
- **D** 9

---

3 10 ÷ ___ = 2
- **A** 5
- **B** 3
- **C** 2
- **D** 9

---

4 14 ÷ ___ = 2
- **A** 8
- **B** 7
- **C** 2
- **D** 5

---

5 10 ÷ ___ = 10
- **A** 1
- **B** 0
- **C** 5
- **D** 15

Directions: Complete each problem.

Example:

26 ÷ 4 = ___
- **A** 105
- **B** 5 r 1
- **C** 4 r 5
- **D** 6 r 2

Answer:

D 6 r 2

---

6 ___ ÷ 10 = 3 r 2
- **A** 30
- **B** 22
- **C** 32
- **D** 5

SAMPLE PRACTICE TEST

7 $7 \div 2 =$ ___
    A   4 r 1
    B   4 r 2
    C   4
    D   3 r 1

8 $4 \overline{) 22}$
    A   5 r 2
    B   2 r 2
    C   10
    D   4 r 2

9 $2 \overline{) 47}$
    A   10 r 1
    B   4 r 1
    C   8
    D   23 r 1

10 $4 \overline{) 15}$
    A   3
    B   3 r 3
    C   2 r 2
    D   6

STOP

FRACTIONS

Directions: Choose the correct answer for each of the following problems.

Example:

$\frac{1}{3} + \frac{1}{3} = $ ___

A $\frac{1}{3}$

B $\frac{2}{3}$

C $\frac{3}{3}$

D none of the above

Answer:

B $\frac{2}{3}$

1 $\frac{1}{4} + \frac{2}{4} = $ ___

A $\frac{1}{5}$

B $\frac{2}{5}$

C $\frac{3}{4}$

D $\frac{4}{5}$

2 $\frac{8}{10} - \frac{2}{10} = $ ___

A $\frac{10}{10}$ B $\frac{6}{10}$

C $\frac{7}{10}$ D $\frac{4}{10}$

3 $\frac{5}{6} - \frac{2}{6}$

A $\frac{3}{6}$

B $\frac{1}{6}$

C $\frac{2}{6}$

D $\frac{4}{6}$

4 $\frac{2}{3} + \frac{2}{3}$

A $\frac{3}{3}$

B $\frac{2}{3}$

C $\frac{4}{3}$

D $\frac{1}{3}$

GO →

5 $\frac{3}{16} + \frac{7}{16} = $ ___

A $\frac{6}{16}$

B $\frac{10}{16}$

C $\frac{8}{16}$

D $\frac{2}{16}$

6 Choose the correct order from *largest* to *smallest* in the following fractions.

A ¼, ⅓, ½

B ⅓, ½, ¼

C ½, ⅓, ¼

D none of the above

7 What fraction does the shaded part of this figure show?

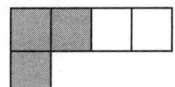

A ⅖

B ⅗

C 5.5

D ¾

8 What fraction does the shaded part of this figure show?

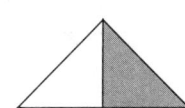

A 1   B ½
C ¼   D ⅔

9 Choose the correct sign to complete this problem: ½ ___ ¼.

A =

B <

C >

D not given

10 Choose the correct sign to complete this problem: ⅓ ___ ½.

A =

B <

C >

D not given

11 Choose the correct sign to complete this problem: 2/4 ___ ½.

A =

B <

C >

D not given

12 Jim and Cindy bought a pizza. If they cut a line down the middle, how much would each person get?

A half

B quarter

C third

D not given

DECIMALS

Directions: Solve each problem below.

Example:

In the number 40.53, what number is in the *tenths* place?

A 0

B 5

C 4

D 2

Answer:

B 5

---

1. For the number 39.84, what number is in the *tenths* place?

   A 4

   B 3

   C 8

   D 9

---

2. What is the number name for five hundred forty-three and twenty-nine hundredths?

   A 534.029

   B 543.2

   C 534.29

   D none of the above

---

3. Write the fraction and the decimal for the shaded area in the figure below.

   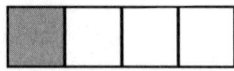

   A ¼ or .25

   B ⅓ or .1

   C ⁴⁄₁₀ or .04

   D none of the above

---

4. Add $8.00 and $3.68.

   A $8.68

   B About $9.00

   C $8.685

   D none of the above

---

5. You bought a baseball glove at a flea market for $2.75. You gave the cashier a $10 bill. How much change did you receive?

   A $8.25

   B About $5.00

   C $7.25

   D none of the above

SAMPLE PRACTICE TEST

6 Solve the problem: 6.4 + 1.2 = ___.
  A 7.42
  B 5.2
  C 6.412
  D 7.6

7 12.034
      +1.342
  A 13.376
  B 12.376
  C 9.692
  D none of the above

8 345.010
      −97.609
  A 247.401
  B 348.401
  C 348. 409
  D 248.619

9 945.50
      −21.60
  A 966.10
  B 967.10
  C 923.90
  D 924.90

10 12.034
        6.980
       +1.342
  A 30.356
  B 20.356
  C 20.456
  D 20.366

MONEY

Directions: Read the following problems and select the correct answer.

Example:

$12.00
0.45
+3.16

A $14.61
B $15.61
C $15.51
D $25.61

Answer:

B $15.61

---

1 $9.05
   +6.98

A $16.93
B $15.93
C $16.13
D $16.03

---

2 $12.00
   −6.05

A $6.05
B $6.95
C $5.95
D none of the above

---

3 Choose the correct position of the letter *h* in the alphabet.
A eleventh
B tenth
C ninth
D eighth

---

4 Choose the numbers that come before and after 4,000.
A 3,999 and 4,001
B 3,900 and 4,100
C 3,901 and 4,010
D 3,990 and 4,110

---

5 Count the money pictured below, and choose the correct value.

A $10.15
B $15.15
C $11.15
D $11.25

SAMPLE PRACTICE TEST

6 Round $5.39 to the nearest dollar.
   - **A** $6.00
   - **B** $5.00
   - **C** $6.50
   - **D** $5.40

7 You buy some candy for $1.23. You give the sales clerk a $5 bill. Choose the correct amount of change you will receive.
   - **A** $3.57
   - **B** $2.43
   - **C** $3.23
   - **D** $3.77

8 You get a $5 allowance every week. You are saving up to buy a video game for $16.50. How many weeks will you have to save to have enough money to buy the game?
   - **A** 3 weeks
   - **B** 4 weeks
   - **C** 5 weeks
   - **D** 6 weeks

9 $2.57 means what?
   - **A** 257 cents
   - **B** 2 dollars and 57 cents
   - **C** 20 dollars and 57 cents
   - **D** not given

10 Ten pennies have a value of what?
   - **A** 100 cents or 2 nickels
   - **B** 10 cents or 10 dimes
   - **C** 10 cents or 1 dime
   - **D** 100 cents or 4 nickels

11 Find the total cost for a soccer ball at $18.59, a baseball mitt at $12.23, and a football at $23.48.
   - **A** $54.30
   - **B** $64.30
   - **C** $74.30
   - **D** $64.60

12 Sarah wants to buy a book that costs $2.25. She has $1.15. How much more money does she need in order to buy the book?
   - **A** $1.10
   - **B** $2.10
   - **C** $1.15
   - **D** none of the above

STOP

GEOMETRY

Directions: Read the following problems and select the correct answer.

Example: What kind of an angle do the hands of a clock make at 9:00?

    A a right angle

    B less than a right angle

    C greater than a right angle

    D none of the above

Answer:

    A a right angle

---

1 Choose the cube from among the shapes pictured below.

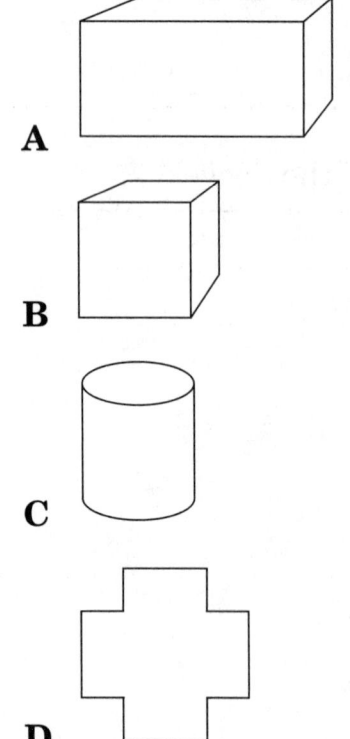

---

2 How many sides does this figure below have?

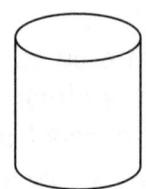

    A 3

    B 4

    C 6

    D 5

---

3 Which one of these figures is *not* a closed shape?

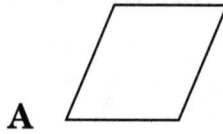

A

B

C

D

4 This figure is a what?

    --------→

    A line segment

    B line

    C ray

    D angle

---

5 Complete the following pattern:

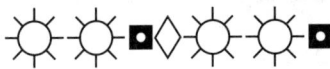

    A ■

    B ◇

    C ■◇

    D ☼☼

---

6 Which figure below shows a correct line of symmetry?

    A

    B

    C

    D

---

7 Choose the figure that is a sphere.

    A

    B

    C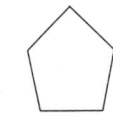

    D STOP

---

8 What is this shape?

    A triangle

    B pentagon

    C octagon

    D hexagon

---

9 Look at this picture. How many units are shown in the rectangle?

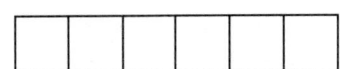

    A 12 units

    B 8 units

    C 6 units

    D 10 units

Directions: Read the following questions and select the correct answer for each one.

Example:

What is the area of this shape? (Area = length × width.)

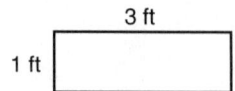

A 6 square feet

B 2 square feet

C 3 square feet

D 6 square inches

Answer:

C 3 square feet

---

10 What is the area of this shape?

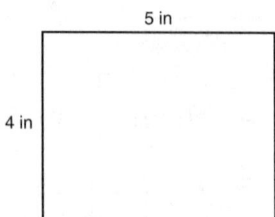

A 20 square inches

B 9 square inches

C 16 square inches

D 18 square inches

---

11 What is the perimeter of this shape?

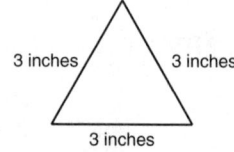

A 4 inches

B 12 inches

C 8 inches

D 9 inches

---

12 Which container is the best one to fill up a 5-quart soup pot the quickest?

A a teaspoon

B a pint jar

C a quart jar

D a measuring cup

---

13 How many suns would fit around the perimeter of the shape below?

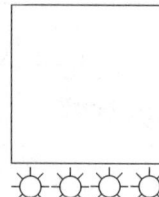

A 8 suns

B 14 suns

C 16 suns

D 6 suns

SAMPLE PRACTICE TEST

14 Which shape has no corners or angles?

A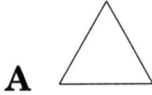

B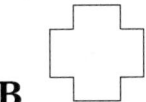

C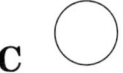

D

15 Which of the figures below is a line segment?

A
B
C
D none of the above

16 Which of the figures below contains only right angles?

A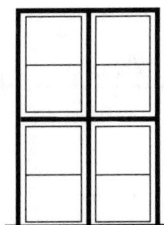

B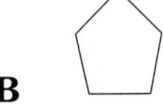

C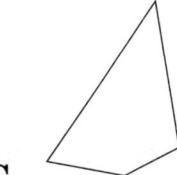

D

117

MEASUREMENT

Directions: Solve each problem below.

Example:

A yard is how many feet?

A 6

B 8

C 3

D 24

Answer:

C 3

---

1. How many inches are there in a yard?

   A 12 inches

   B 108 inches

   C 24 inches

   D none of the above

2. How many feet equal 4 yards?

   A 9 feet

   B 12 feet

   C 6 feet

   D none of the above

3. How many yards are equal to 6 feet?

   A 2 yards

   B 5 yards

   C 4 yards

   D none of the above

4. How many yards are equal to 12 inches?

   A ⅓ yard

   B ¼ yards

   C 3 yards

   D none of the above

5. Would you measure a football field in inches or yards?

   A inches

   B yards

   C neither

6. Which is more, 2 pints or 1 quart?

   A 2 pints

   B 1 quart

   C They are equal.

7. How would you measure a safety pin?

   A in centimeters

   B in yards

   C in feet

   D in miles

GO →

8 Which is more, 1 quart or 1 cup?
   A 1 cup
   B 1 quart
   C They are equal.

Directions: Solve each problem.

Example:

Mrs. Smith bought 12 quarts of milk this week. How many pints of milk is this?
   A 23
   B 24
   C 12
   D 48

Answer:
   B 24

9 The gas tank in John's car holds 15 gallons. It took 10 gallons to fill the tank. How many gallons were in the tank before it was filled?
   A 10
   B 5
   C 15
   D 2

10 Betty bought 12 liters of soda. The soda was in four bottles of the same size. How many liters of soda were in each bottle?
   A 1
   B 4
   C 3
   D 6

11 Shannon uses 2 gallons of gas to mow a lawn. She mowed the lawn 13 times this summer. How much gas did she use to mow the lawn this summer?
   A 36 gallons
   B 26 gallons
   C 13 gallons
   D 2 gallons

12 One liter is a little _____ than a quart.
   A more
   B less
   C about the same
   D none of the above

13 Pete bought 2 yards of fishing line for his rod. How many feet did he buy?
   A 3 feet
   B 6 feet
   C 2 feet
   D 1 feet

14 About how many liters would a sink hold if it were full?
   A 1 liter
   B 10 liters
   C 200 liters
   D none of the above

15 If a thermometer in the freezer read 82°F, is this too cold, too hot, or just about right?

  A Too cold

  B Too hot

  C Just about right

MATH, GRADE THREE

Answer Key for Sample Practice Test

Addition
1. B
2. D
3. A
4. C
5. C
6. A
7. C
8. A
9. B
10. B
11. C
12. D
13. B
14. D
15. C
16. A

Subtraction
1. D
2. A
3. B
4. A
5. C
6. A
7. D
8. A
9. A
10. B
11. B
12. A
13. A
14. A
15. A
16. B

Multiplication
1. C
2. C
3. D
4. C
5. C
6. D
7. B
8. D
9. B
10. C
11. A
12. D
13. B
14. B
15. A
16. D

Division
1. C
2. C
3. A
4. B
5. A
6. C
7. D
8. A
9. D
10. B

Fractions
1. C
2. B
3. A
4. C
5. B
6. C
7. B
8. B
9. C
10. B
11. A
12. A

Decimals
1. C
2. D
3. A
4. D
5. C
6. D
7. A
8. A
9. C
10. B

Money
1. D
2. C
3. D
4. A
5. C
6. B
7. D
8. B
9. B
10. C
11. A
12. A

Geometry
1. B
2. A
3. B
4. C
5. B
6. D
7. A
8. B
9. C
10. A
11. D
12. C
13. C
14. C
15. C
16. A

Measurement
1. D
2. B
3. A
4. A
5. B
6. C
7. A
8. B
9. B
10. C
11. B
12. A
13. B
14. B
15. B

WORKSHEET

WORKSHEET

WORKSHEET

WORKSHEET

WORKSHEET

WORKSHEET

WORKSHEET

WORKSHEET

WORKSHEET

WORKSHEET

WORKSHEET

WORKSHEET